CONCORDIA UNIV.
PN6120.C5C5141977   C001 V
CHRISTMAS PLAYS FOR YOUNG PLAYERS

3 4211 000073640

T4-AEA-677

WITHDRAWN

*Christmas Plays
for
Young Players*

Also by MAXINE McSWEENY:

Creative Children's Theatre for Home, School, Church, and Playground

Christmas Plays for Young Players

Maxine McSweeny

South Brunswick and New York: A. S. Barnes and Company
London: Thomas Yoseloff Ltd

©1977 by A. S. Barnes and Co., Inc.

A. S. Barnes and Co., Inc.
Cranbury, New Jersey 08512

Thomas Yoseloff Ltd.
Magdalen House
136-148 Tooley Street
London SE1 2TT, England

Library of Congress Cataloging in Publication Data
Main entry under title:
Christmas plays for young players.

CONTENTS: Holbrook, M. The toymaker's doll.--
McSweeny, M. Listen to the peace and goodwill.--
Cavanah, F. The transfiguration of the gifts. [etc.]
1. Christmas plays. I. McSweeny, Maxine.
PN6120.C5C514   1977   808.82'9'33   76-18480
ISBN 0-498-01959-4

PRINTED IN THE UNITED STATES OF AMERICA

Contents

Introduction	7
The Toymaker's Doll By Marion Holbrook	11
Listen to the Peace and Goodwill By Maxine McSweeny	37
The Transfiguration of the Gifts By Frances Cavanah	59
The Least of These By Ella Wilson and Anna Field	77
Santa! Please Get Up! By Maxine McSweeny	99
The Christmas Party By Maxine McSweeny	123

Introduction

"May we give a Christmas play?" Every year children and teenagers ask this question of their school and Sunday school teachers, club leaders, playground directors, or parents. These leaders need plays that challenge the interest and suit the skill of young players and result in a good performance. The plays in this book have often answered such need. Many leaders have used them with success for both players and audience.

These six plays vary in theme and setting as they portray various aspects of the many-sided holiday that is Christmas. Santa Claus and the Martians are central characters in an ultramodern comedy. There is a nativity play about children who visited the manger on that first Christmas Eve. These are for the six- to ten-year-olds. Plays for older groups show dramatic situations in which Christmas helped people meet crises in their lives.

Each play tells an interesting story that builds to an exciting climax that young people have brought to life on the stage. Although most of the plays offer parts for ten to twenty players this number can be reduced. Group songs and dances that increase the appeal of some plays give opportunity for more participants.

All the plays are short, ranging in playing time from fifteen to thirty minutes. Stage settings and costumes are simple and may be achieved with easy-to-obtain materials. The six plays may be presented in a classroom, clubroom, living room, or chancel of a church as well as in an auditorium. No front curtain is necessary. Success of these plays depends not on their settings but on the sincere and enthusiastic acting of young players.

An American philosopher once said, "America needs more holidays, and then, she needs to know what to do with them." The six plays in this book give young people something to do for Christmas that offers them education as well as holiday fun.

*Christmas Plays
for
Young Players*

The Toymaker's Doll

by Marion Holbrook

CHARACTERS:

FRANZ BROCK, the toymaker
MINNA, his wife
HILDA, his granddaughter
THE BURGOMASTER
CHRISTINA, a poor woman
THE WOMAN, a stranger
A MESSENGER from the Prince
SHEPHERDESS
DANCER
SOLDIERS
THE CHILDREN of the neighborhood

TIME: *Christmas Eve.*

SCENE: *The workshop of Franz Brock. There is an entrance down right that leads to the street, another down left that leads to the kitchen. There is a rough worktable left center with a bench or stool at its right. A chair is right center. On the worktable are wooden blocks, knives, chisels, and various implements. There is an opening, supposed to be a cupboard up right center. It is coverd with curtains or a screen. Across the back of the stage except in front of the cupboard, and along the walls right and left are tables, shelves, and cabinets displaying toys of all kinds.*

AT RISE OF CURTAIN: *The stage is empty. Children's voices, singing carols, are heard as from a distance off right. Hilda enters left, crosses to the door right, and looks out. Minna enters left.*

MINNA: What is it, Hilda? Is your Grandfather coming?
HILDA: No, Grandmother. It's the children. They're singing their carols. (*She sighs.*)
MINNA: What is it, dear? Surely my little Hilda is not sad on Christmas Eve.
HILDA (*wistfully*): No—it's nothing. (*But she sighs again.*)
MINNA: But there is something. Tell me.
HILDA: It's the children, Grandmother. They'll be coming here in a little—
MINNA: Of course they will. To sing their carols.
HILDA: And—and—to see if Grandfather has any toys for them.
MINNA: Oh—that—is so—
HILDA: And Grandfather is so changed.
MINNA: (*sighing, too*): I know.
HILDA: Sometimes I wish he'd never invented the dolls.
MINNA: (*shocked*): Hilda!
HILDA: But I do! We were happier when we were poor! Then we always had something to give to everyone. And now, when we're rich—
(*Franz Brock bustles importantly in right.*)
MINNA: Here you are, Franz!
FRANZ: (*taking off his wraps as he hurries to his chair and picks up his work, a little toy soldier*): Yes, yes, and in a hurry, too!

HILDA: Grandfather, did you hear the children singing?
FRANZ (*impatiently*): Yes, yes, of course. How could I help it? They were jamming the square til I thought I'd never get through. And me with a thousand things to do!
HILDA: Grandfather, when the children come —
FRANZ: Run along, now, Hilda. Grandfather has work to do. *(Hilda starts to speak again, but Minna shakes her head and nods toward the entrance left.)*
(Hilda with a troubled look at Franz tiptoes out left.)
FRANZ: *(pausing and placing the soldier with others on the table):* Minna, look!
MINNA *(crossing up center)*: Yes, Franz. What is it?
FRANZ *(with a gesture toward the soldiers)*: Look at them, Minna. Did you ever see finer soldiers? A round dozen of them, and each as perfect as the Bishop's prayers.
MINNA *(regarding the soldiers thoughtfully)*: Perhaps. But they look no better to me than the soldiers you made last Christmas, or the year before that.
FRANZ: *(impatiently)*: Of course they're no different! But think, Minna! Think! Last year they were merely the handiwork of Poor old Franz, the toymaker. They went begging on my shelves, or sold for a penny each. Ah, but this year — they are made by Franz, the famous toymaker! Franz, who is known from here to the mountains and from here to the sea! And why? Because I'm the only toy-

MINNA: maker in the kingdom — in the whole world for all I know — who can make a walking doll!

MINNA: Yes, it's true. It was clever of you, Franz, to make those dolls, and God knows they've brought us riches. *(But she sighs and shakes her head.)*

FRANZ: They'll bring us more than riches, Minna. Think of it! Fame! Fame, I said!

MINNA: I heard you, Franz.

FRANZ: Woman, don't you understand what that means? No more slaving, no more doffing the cap, no more insults from innkeepers and such. And all by the honest work of my hands and the cleverness of my brain. I wouldn't wonder, Minna, if I should become dollmaker for the children of the king, himself. What a change since last year! Eh, my Minna?

MINNA *(slowly)*: Yes. Last year we sat down to our bread with grateful hearts.

FRANZ: And got up from the table with empty stomachs.

MINNA *(not heeding him)*: You made many a poor child happy, Franz, by giving away the leftover toys. And many a poor mother blessed you for it. Ah, no. It isn't like last year.

FRANZ: Minna, you can't eat blessings. 'Twas like throwing good money down a well. My dolls have changed all that — my wonderful walking dolls!

MINNA: Yes, your dolls have changed all that — *(The sound of the carols is heard again and draws near.)*

MINNA *(anxiously)*: Franz, it's the children!

The Toymaker's Doll

FRANZ: Yes, Yes! Tell them to go away and be still. I must get work done!

MINNA: But Franz, they always come on Christmas Eve! You always give them toys.!

FRANZ: Woman, do you think the shop of Franz, the most famous toymaker in all the land, is to be overrun with little beggars! Tell them to go away!

(Shaking her head sadly, Minna crosses to the entrance right. Before she can stop them the children pour in, a happy avalanche dancing about her.)

ALL THE CHILDREN *(in a happy jumble of greetings):* Merry Christmas, Grandmother Minna! Merry Christmas, Grandfather Franz! Did you hear our carols? We came straight to see you. We come every year, don't we?

MINNA *(anxiously shushing them, with her finger to her lips):* Ssh! Grandfather is very busy!

FIRST CHILD: But it's Christmas Eve!

SECOND CHILD: We always come on Christmas Eve!

THIRD CHILD: He always gives us toys!

FOURTH CHILD: A doll with some paint off —

FIFTH CHILD: Or a whistle that doesn't blow very much.

SIXTH CHILD: I got a whistle last year, and it blew fine when I fixed it.

SEVENTH CHILD: May I have a little doll for my baby sister?

EIGHTH CHILD: Is there something that winds up and goes? I like things that go! If it's a little bit broken, I can fix it. Mother says I'm handy with my hands.

NINTH CHILD: So am I! I can fix toys. I'm going to be a toymaker when I grow up.

ALL CHILDREN: So am I! A toymaker! I'll be a famous toymaker! *(almost shouting)* We'll be a whole

town full of toymakers!
(Minna tries in vain to quiet the children, and at last Franz rises and calls out impatiently.)

FRANZ: Silence! Silence! How do you think I can work in this noise?

TENTH CHILD: Forgive us, Grandfather Franz. We'll wait till you're done working!

ELEVENTH CHILD: We'll be just as still!

TWELFTH CHILD: Just as still as little mice.

THIRTEENTH CHILD: *(trying to sound like a mouse):* Eek! Eek! *(The Children giggle irrepressibly, then they are silent again.)*

FOURTEENTH CHILD: May we look at the toys while we're waiting?

FRANZ *(settling to his work again):* If you don't touch them.

FIFTEENTH CHILD: Couldn't I wind up just one and make it go?

SIXTEENTH CHILD: Couldn't I blow a little toot on a horn?

SEVENTEENTH CHILD: Couldn't I cuddle a little dolly? A little soft one? And put my cheek against her?

FRANZ *(stubbornly)*: No! You may look at the toys if you're quiet. But mind you, you keep your hands behind you! Do you hear me?
(Children nod mutely and clasp their hands behind them.)

FRANZ: A single Meddlesome Mattie, and out you go, every one of you!

(The Children, very much subdued, tiptoe about, looking longingly at the toys, bending close to them, forgetting their hands, and almost touching them, and then jerking away from them. The Woman enters right silently and watches Franz and the children. Franz does not see her. The children look at her fearfully and edge away from her. She crosses up left and stands motionless. Children give her very wide berth when they pass her, looking at the toys.)

ALL CHILDREN *(talking among themselves)*: Who is she? I'm scared. I'm not. I'm not a bit afraid.

(Christina enters right)

CHRISTINA: Good day, Toymaker.

FRANZ *(glancing up quickly, and then looking down indifferently)*: Well, my good woman, what do you want?

CHRISTINA: A toy. Just a little toy, sir, for a small child.

FRANZ *(indifferently)*: Well, you see what I have. Look around and make your choice.

(Christina looks longingly at the toys, occasionally touching one.)

MINNA *(pleading)*: Franz—

FRANZ: Minna, go and see if the wood has come. I must finish that doll before night. It's getting late, and the Burgomaster may buy it if it's done. *(Lowering his voice)* It'll mean another gold piece in my purse.

MINNA: Yes, Franz. I'll find more wood—for more dolls—and more gold—though God knows what need we have of more gold.

(Minna goes out left, shaking her head disapprovingly.)

CHRISTINA: Are you the toymaker who makes the walking dolls?
FRANZ: I am.
CHRISTINA: Could I see one of them?
(Children murmur excitedly until Franz silences them with a scowl.)
FRANZ: You wish to buy one of my dolls?
CHRISTINA: No. Oh, no! I'm too poor. But my little Gretchen is ill and talks of nothing but the walking dolls. I thought if I could tell her how it moves, how it is dressed, and if its curls are flaxen or brown, it might quiet her.
(Again the Children murmur excitedly, and Franz scowls, and they subside.)
FRANZ: You ask me to start the delicate machinery of a valuable doll to satisfy a notion?
CHRISTINA: It's only that my Gretchen is so ill. I thought—Wouldn't it be possible?
FRANZ: I couldn't do that. How do I know you're not a spy, come to learn the secrets of my trade? No. I couldn't risk it.
CHRISTINA: You're a hard man to say that, Franz Brock.
FRANZ *(sternly):* Be that as it may. Perhaps some little toy would please your child. I have many of small value here.
CHRISTINA: Alas, I've no money. Perhaps you have a broken toy—a small doll that was spoiled in the making—or a little wooden lamb—or anything.
FRANZ: That I could give you for nothing?
(Christina nods eagerly.)
FRANZ *(knitting his brows):* I might—of course I could not sell it. But, no. It would start all the rabble of

the town coming here for favors. No, I'm sorry, but I cannot give you anything.

CHRISTINA *(gives him a long, steady look):* Franz Brock, there was a time when you sympathized with poor folk. When you were poor yourself. I pray God you'll never have need of sympathy.!

(Christina goes out right. The Children murmur aloud in sympathy.)

ALL THE CHILDREN *(talking together):* Poor woman! Poor little girl! She's so sick! She ought to have one little toy.

(Hilda enters left with a basket of blocks of wood.)

FIRST CHILD: *(forgetting and picking up a little doll):* Look, Grandfather Franz! This doll is broken! Couldn't I run and give it to the poor woman?

FRANZ *(impatiently):* There! What did I tell you? The first Meddlesome Mattie, and out you all go!

ALL THE CHILDREN *(protesting together):* But we didn't touch anything. We have minded! We've been just as still! We won't touch anything else!

FRANZ *(sternly):* Out you go! Every one of you!
(Disappointed, with hanging heads, the Children tiptoe outdoors right.)

HILDA: Grandfather! You're not sending the children away! Not on Christmas Eve!

FRANZ: I'm busy.

HILDA: But Grandfather—

FRANZ: Hilda, be quiet!

HILDA *(frightened, shrinking back down right):* Yes, Grandfather—

(Franz turns and for the first time notices The Woman.)

FRANZ *(returning to his chair):* Well, my good woman, what can I do for you?

THE WOMAN: *(sternly):* Nothing.

FRANZ: Then why are you here?

THE WOMAN: I came to see if certain things are true.

FRANZ: What things?

THE WOMAN: Word of you has traveled far and wide.

FRANZ: You come from the Prince? Has the Prince heard of my dolls?

THE WOMAN: I come from someone far more important than the Prince. Someone who is very much displeased with you.

FRANZ: Displeased with me? The cleverest toymaker in all the country?

THE WOMAN: Displeased with you, the most selfish man in all the country.

FRANZ: Selfish? I?

THE WOMAN *(solemnly):* Franz Brock, your heart has become as hard as the gold you love. But there is one thing you still love more than gold.

FRANZ: Of course there is! My little granddaughter! I do everything for her. That's why I work so hard and save. To have more for her. Isn't that it, Hilda?

(Hilda does not answer.)

FRANZ *(sternly):* Hilda!

HILDA *(frightened):* Yes, Grandfather!

THE WOMAN: You have not made her happy.

FRANZ: Not happy! Of course she's happy. Aren't you, HIlda?

(Hilda hangs her head.)

FRANZ *(giving a command, not asking a question):* Hilda! Aren't you happy?

HILDA *(quickly):* Yes, Grandfather.
FRANZ: There! Did you hear her?
THE WOMAN: I heard her.
FRANZ: You think I should still be just old Franz, the toymaker, who gave away things at Christmas because he couldn't sell them. Hah!
THE WOMAN: Franz Brock, before this Christmas Eve is over, you will give away anything—everything.
FRANZ: I? Give away everything? You're a poor crazed creature, or I'd have you locked up for your threats. Go along now, for I have important work to do.
(Franz settles to his work. The Woman stalks past him to the entrance. There she turns and speaks as though casting a spell.)
THE WOMAN *(solemnly):* Remember! You will gladly give away all you have.
(The Woman goes out right.)
HILDA: What did she mean?
FRANZ: Nothing at all. Bring me the blocks of wood.
HILDA: I'm frightened. She looked at me so strangely.
FRANZ: Forget about her. Come, run along now, for I'm very busy.
(Hilda sets the basket of wood on the table. Franz chooses a block and begins working. Hilda stands beside him. There is an instant of silence.)
HILDA: Grandfather—
FRANZ: I told you to run along!
HILDA *(crossing to the left entrance)*: But—I—I—did want to say one thing.

FRANZ: Well?

HILDA (*slowly*): I wish—you hadn't sent the children away.
(*Hilda goes out left. Franz looks after Hilda, then shrugs and returns to his work.*)
(*Burgomaster comes in right. Franz scrambles to his feet.*)

FRANZ: Good evening to you, sir! Good evening! It is always an honor to have the Burgomaster walk into my shop.

BURGOMASTER: Good evening, Brock. How about the dolls? Are they ready?

FRANZ (*pulling his chair below the table*): They are ready, sir. Only seat yourself and permit me to show them to you. And I have still another almost finished. You will take that one, too, eh?

BURGOMASTER: But I'm already buying three soldiers, a French dancing doll, and a shepherdess! Keep the other in readiness, Brock. It wouldn't surprise me if the Prince heard of you.

FRANZ: The Prince, you say! What makes you think that?

BURGOMASTER: It would do the good name of the town no harm if the Prince came here to buy from our famous toymaker. I've sent one of the dolls to my nephew in the city. He is close to a friend of the Prince. Who knows what may come of that?

FRANZ: Ah, who knows, indeed! How can I thank you, sir?

BURGOMASTER: Tut, tut. I'm thinking of our town as well as you. Bring out the dolls, man. I'm al-

	ready late for supper. *(He seats himself. Franz goes to the cupboard that is covered with the curtains or screen and brings out the Soldier Dolls. Burgomaster leans forward eagerly.)*
BURGOMASTER:	Wonderful, Brock! Wonderful! And do they move like the others?
FRANZ:	Only wait! I'll show you.

(Franz winds the Soldier Dolls. The First Soldier moves slightly, then the Second, and when others are wound, they march stiffly to the tune of a tinkling march. They march around the shop and then slow down near the outside entrance.)

BURGOMASTER *(as excited as a child):* Excellent! Now the dancers! Show me the dancers!

(Franz escorts the Dancers from the cupboard. They walk stiffly as he seems to push them. When they're wound, dainty waltz music is heard, and they dance. While the toys are performing Franz looks on with great pride.)

BURGOMASTER: You are a genius, Brock. And now the Shepherdess.

(Franz brings out the Shepherdess. He winds her, and she dances. Gradually she runs down, making her last curtsy before Burgomaster.)

BURGOMASTER: *(laughing):* The vixen is bewitched. Here! *(handing Franz a purse.)* Your price is high, but for such skill one pays willingly.

FRANZ *(humbly):* Thank you, sir.

BURGOMASTER: I'll go now and take the dolls with me. My cart is waiting outside.

(Franz quickly winds the dolls and gives them a push toward the entrance right. They walk out woodenly. Burgomaster follows them.)

BURGOMASTER: *(at the door):* Good night, Brock! And a Merry Christmas to you!

FRANZ: Thank you. Thank you. A Merry Christmas to you, sir.

(Burgomaster goes out right. Franz stands counting his money.)

FRANZ: Gold! I shall make more dolls and have more gold. Who knows where it may end?

(There is a loud rap at the door right, and the Messenger enters.)

FRANZ *(startled by the Messenger's sudden appearance):* Blessed saints! Good evening, sir!

MESSENGER: I am sent by His Royal Highness, the Prince, to purchase one of your walking dolls, Herr Brock.

FRANZ: One of my dolls. The Prince wants one of my dolls! *(He rushes to the door right, calling.)* Burgomaster! Burgomaster! Wait! Come back! *(He turns back.)* He's gone. The Burgomaster has taken the last of my dolls.

MESSENGER: Then you have no doll to sell to the Prince?

FRANZ *(beside himself with regret):* I have one, but it is not quite finished. Oh, sir, could you come back within an hour? I shall have it ready then, I swear to you.

MESSENGER: Men do not ask the Prince to wait an hour. He has never waited five minutes for anyone. I shall have to tell him that the toymaker prefers to deal with burgomasters.

The Toymaker's Doll

FRANZ: Oh, no! No, no, no! Don't tell him that. Wait! Wait! Sit down! I shall go to work at once.
(Franz snatches a block of wood from the basket, picks up his knife, and starts to carve while the Messenger folds his arms and watches Franz haughtily.)

FRANZ: It's all done but the head, you see. It will take no time at all to finish it.
(Franz whittles and carves nervously for a moment. Then a cry is heard off stage. Franz drops his knife, and the Messenger looks up startled.)
(Minna enters left.)

MINNA: Husband! Husband! A terrible thing has happened!

FRANZ: Minna, what is it? Has someone stolen my money?

MINNA: The fiends take your money! It's Hilda, Franz! Hilda!

FRANZ: Hilda?

MINNA *(clutching him in fright and pointing off left)*: Look! Look! See for yourself. It is a curse laid on us. It is a punishment.
(Franz, Minna, and the Messenger stand looking off left.)
(Hilda enters left. She has turned into a doll. The click of the doll's mechanism is heard as she walks jerkily into the room, her eyes vacant and her face in the fixed expression of a doll.)

FRANZ: Hilda! *(in fright)* Minna, she is a doll!
(Minna covers her face with her hands. Hilda crosses to the chair right and falls

into it in the sprawling, stiff position of a doll. The Messenger looks at her with intrest.)

MESSENGER: Exquisite! Why did you lie to me, old man. Upon my oath I never saw a fairer doll! What's your price?

MINNA *(astonished):* What does he say?

FRANZ: She's not a doll! I swear to you, it's my own granddaughter!

MESSENGER: Come, old man, no tricks to raise your price. The Prince is a fair man, but no one ever got the better of him. What will you take?

MINNA *(bewildered):* The Prince?

FRANZ: Minna, the Prince himself has sent for a walking doll.

MINNA: He wants to buy—Hilda?

FRANZ: Yes, Minna. Yes.

MINNA *(going to Messenger):* Go back to the Prince and tell him we have no doll for sale. Tell him he may take our lives if it is his will, but say that Franz Brock has no walking dolls for sale! Oh, we are strangely cursed, good sir. She is in truth our grandchild.

MESSENGER *(amused):* A maiden bewitched into a doll?

MINNA: It is our own Hilda.

MESSENGER: You must be mad. I never heard of such a thing. Then you will not sell the doll? Not for so much as ten gold pieces?

FRANZ: Ten gold pieces! No, not for all the kingdom!

MESSENGER: As you will, Herr Brock. I shall say that the toymaker is a madman.

FRANZ: A madman. Yes.

The Toymaker's Doll

(Messenger makes a gesture of scorn and goes out right.)

MINNA *(sobbing):* Oh, Franz! What shall we do?

FRANZ: I don't know! I don't know.

(The sound of carols is heard softly in the distance.)

FRANZ: Poor little Hilda! I made her say she was happy. And she didn't mean it. The last thing she said to me was, "I wish you hadn't sent the children away." *(He crosses to where Hilda sits, staring unblinkingly.)* Hilda, Grandfather's sorry.

(The sound of carols draws nearer.)

MINNA *(softly):* Franz, the children!

FRANZ: Yes, yes — the children! Tell them to come in, Minna. Tell them Grandfather Franz wants them.

(Minna crosses right and goes out.)

FRANZ *(turning to Hilda again):* The old woman knew, little Granddaughter. She said before the night was over, I'd gladly give away all I have. And now, when it's too late to make you happy, I give away the toys.

(Minna enters right, followed by the Children. They are hanging back a little timidly.)

MINNA: Come. Come. Grandfather Franz sent for you. He has toys for you. For every one of you. Franz, you're glad to see the children, aren't you?

FRANZ *(turning from Hilda and mustering up a smile and stretching out his hands to them):* My little children! Come to see old Grandfather Franz!

(The Children, happy again, dance about and shout with joy.)

ALL THE
CHILDREN: Franz! Grandfather Franz! Greetings. Grandfather Franz! Greetings, Grandmother Minna! Have you toys for us? Have you a doll for me, Grandfather Franz? Is there a horn? Will you let me have a whistle?

FRANZ *(while the Children are still babbling)*: Welcome, little ones! Come in, come in. What can Grandfather Franz give you? What will you have, little friends? Everything in my shop is yours.

(Children gather around him, shouting and laughing. Others continue to sing and carol. Franz and Minna distribute toys, talking to Children as they do so. Children receive their gifts with cries of thanks.)

FRANZ AND MINNA *(as they distribute the toys)*: Something for everyone. Ah, it is good to have you in my shop again. This is for you, and this is for you. Here is a whistle. Take it and welcome. Dolls? You shall have dolls. Soldiers? Here, my lad. Here, little maiden. Skates? You shall have them.

(Several children gather around Hilda, tugging at her.)

CHILDREN: Hilda! Hilda! Come and dance! Come and dance with us, Hilda!

(There is silence as all eyes are turned on Hilda. Children stand at either side of her, so that she can be seen. Slowly Hilda moves. Franz and Minna clasp their hands

HILDA:	*in thankfulness. Hilda looks around in astonishment. She rises, smiling.)* Grandfather! Grandmother! It's the way it used to be on Christmas Eve. I want to dance! I want to dance with the children! I'm so happy! *(Children cluster around Hilda, laughing and singing. They sing and dance, and in conclusion dance off right. Hilda goes with them. Music fades. Franz and Minna stand motionless, listening.)*
MINNA *(softly):*	Franz, isn't it good to hear them singing?
FRANZ:	Yes, it is sweeter than the sound of one gold piece clinking against another — the sound of children singing. *(Offstage singing rises to a climax as Franz and Minna, arm in arm go slowly off left.)* THE END

SUGGESTIONS FOR THE DIRECTOR*

Regarding Rehearsal and Production of *The Toymaker's Doll*

As director of *The Toymaker's Doll* you will find the play appeals to players of a wide age range. Thirteen- and fourteen-year-olds have enjoyed acting the main roles. So have ten-year-olds. In casting the play it is important that those who play Neighborhood Children are shorter than those who play the adults. This is one of the few factors of physical appearance that concern the director in lining up a cast. Casting should provide for emergencies by designation of two players for each

---

*For step-by-step guidance in conducting rehearsals see Maxine McSweeny, *Creative Children's Theatre for Home, School, Church, and Playground* (South Brunswick and New York: A.S. Barnes and Co., 1974), p. 151.

of the main roles, particularly Franz, Minna, and Hilda. Then, schedule more than one performance of the play. This gives opportunity for both the players who have been cast and rehearsed in a role to appear in it before an audience.

One of the advantages of this play is that rehearsals can be scheduled so some of the players do not have long waits while others rehearse. Schedule Franz's scenes with Minna, Hilda, Christina, Strange Woman, Burgomaster, and Messenger fifteen or twenty minues apart during middle rehearsals when players work on characterizaton. All players should be present throughout the first two rehearsals when they are becoming familiar with the play's story, and again, at final rehearsals when they work for smoothness and continuity.

Between the beginning and the final rehearsals you should guide players in bringing their characters to life. First, there is Franz. Help him realize he is the one who makes things happen. Ask this player questions about Franz's attitude toward the different people who enter his shop, and how his attitude changes with the entrance of each visitor. He must understand and portray Franz's irritation at the interruption by the children; his pride as he tells Minna the Prince may buy one of his dolls; his harshness with Christina; his anger when one child picks up a toy. He may even seem to slap the child's hand if he coordinates his movement of striking with a clap of hands by someone offstage. This will be a climactic moment heightened by the recoil of the Children. Franz's anger changes to insolence as he insults the Strange Woman; then to a fawning desire to please when Burgomaster enters; later to frenzy when he argues with Messenger; and to grief and remorse over the enchantment of Hilda. Finally, he shows gentle kindliness to the returning children as he realizes they are more important than gold. The more convincing Franz is, the better will all other players portray their characters.

Children of the neighborhood need special consideration. If you have only a limited number of participants, four or five children can carry the scene almost as well as the seventeen listed in the script. But if you have many who want to participate, the seventeen give more boys and girls a chance to be in the play. Instead of designating Children as First Child, Second Child, etc., let each player choose a name for the child he plays. It is more fun to have a name than a number, and choosing names can provide pleasant activity. The name each player chooses should be written into the scripts, and appear opposite his own on the program if printed programs are used. With these techniques you can make small parts more interesting to players.

Another technique for this purpose and for the good of the production is to schedule special rehearsals of the Children's scenes with Franz. They need to practice so they do not sound like a chorus with all of them saying the same words at the same time. Rather, their speeches on first entrance should sound like the jumble of greetings they are supposed to be. Practice until important speeches are heard above the hubbub as all show their delight in visiting the toyshop. These players also need extra rehearsal of their later scenes so their pantomime and speeches portray successively their desire to play with the toys; their sympathy for Christina; their schock when Franz slaps one child's hand; their disappointment when he sends them away, their joy when he welcomes them back and when Hilda dances away with them.

Plan Children's movement about the stage so they do not stand in one big mass. Let them gather in little groups of twos, threes, even fours. The groups change as Children move in reaction to the play's people and events. Children should understand that such reaction on their part is essential to the play and makes its story logical and exciting to the audience.

The dolls that Franz winds up to dance for Burgomaster learn their dances at times other than regular rehearsals. Only at the last two or three rehearsals do they work with the cast to become familiar with their locations on the stage in relation to other players; and to coordinate their dances with actors' speeches and pantomime.

You may wish to include several dolls of each type instead of the three soldiers, one shepherdess, and one dancer listed in the script. This gives opportunity for more children to participate and adds vitality to the production that solo dances rarely contribute.

You may not have in the group presenting the play enough members to cast several of them as dancers. In this event recruit all the dancers from another club, class, or even agency. Perhaps their leader will teach them the steps of the dances. These steps need be no more involved than running, skipping, and walking, but they should be suited to the type of doll they represent. Then they should be executed with assurance and enthusiasm.

If the types of dolls suggested by the script are not practical in your situation, you will find other types just as effective. Factors influencing your choice are age, sex, and ability of the dancers and problems of costuming them. If you already have costumes suited to certain kinds of dolls, choose the kind of dolls that fit the costumes. Among the variety of dolls which have been successfully chosen are baby dolls, French dolls, rag dolls, clown dolls, and folk dolls of various nationalities. If your production includes several dolls of each type, then Franz should escort each group offstage at the conclusion of its dance. This prevents crowding of players on the stage.

The roles of Minna and Hilda present one or two problems to young actors. You should help Minna with her scream of terror when she first sees Hilda as a doll. Let her practice this with you when no other players are present prior to rehearsing it with the rest of the cast. It may help her to scream a word or phrase like "Oh, no!" or "Look! It's Hilda!" or just "Hilda!" Whatever words are used the sound must carry enough terror to frighten Franz and Messenger on the stage. Hilda will need your help before or after rehearsal so her movements after the enchantment are stiff and mechanical, and her facial expression is set and unchanging.

The roles of Christina, Burgomaster, and Messenger should be easy to interpret. But the Strange Woman is a mystery. Let your players discuss her — who is she? — why is she there? One cast decided she was the Spirit of Christmas. In their production her costume was red and green with a gold tinsel girdle, all of it concealed beneath a dark cape with a hood. Frequently when she turned away from Franz and toward the audience she opened the cape to reveal the shining dress beneath. The same use of a cape was made by another cast. These players interpreted her as the Madonna. Under her dark cape she wore a white dress with a blue girdle. Her cape had no hood. Over her head she wore a soft blue flowing scarf. Others who gave the play agreed that Strange Woman was Franz's guardian angel. Her long dress was white with streamers of gold tinsel flowing from neck to hem. Little gold wings were visible above her shoulders when she lowered her cape. She held her cape, which had no hood, close about her except when Franz was not looking at her. Then she lowered the cape to show her sparkling costume and tiny shining wings to the audience.

Many productions of this play have been effective with a minimum effort at special costuming. Girls and women except Strange Woman wore lightly gathered skirts and pale colored or white blouses. Around their waists were dark bodices that laced up the front. These were made of black interfacing materials like Pellon. They could be made of felt, corduroy, velveteen, or other fabric with body enough to hold its shape. Children of the Neighborhood and Hilda wore short skirts and long stockings (no socks). Christina and Minna wore long skirts.

Men and boys were appropriately dressed in smocks and their own long trousers. Smocks had full sleeves and gathers at the shoulder or at the bottom of a shoulder yoke. One cast had difficulty in getting smocks. They wore their own shirts hanging outside their trousers and with collars open. Around their waists they tied sashes of bright colors. In all productions the smocks of Franz and Neighborhood boys were of cottonlike fabric. Burgomaster wore a similar smock, but his was elaborated with decorative design made of braid or embroidery or applied with crayon or paint. One Burgomaster wore a robe something like a choir robe. It was of deep, rich color and decorated with the same materials as the first Burgomaster's smock.

The Prince's Messenger, of course, wore the most elegant costume of all. Although his trousers were of contemporary style, his smock was of a texture that suggested silk or velvet and was decorated with gold braid or paint. Over it he wore a velvet cape about as long as his smock.

Both Burgomaster and Messenger had berets. Attached to the headband and drooping slightly toward the shoulder each had a feather. The Messenger's was a peacock feather; Burgomaster's was more like a goose quill. If real feathers are hard to get, make them out of a length of wire and several layers of fringed and curled crepe paper.

Almost every character needs headgear. It is particularly important for those who enter from outdoors. Neighborhood Girls wear a varied assortment of kerchiefs and hoods. Neighborhood boys wear stocking caps of various lengths, colors, and textures, Christina wears a shawl over her head and hooked beneath her chin. Franz wears a cape and stocking cap. Although Minna does not come from outdoors, she will look more like a grandmother if she wears a little white cap. One like Whistler's Mother's would be fitting.

Additional ways to make Minna and Franz look older are to brush white powder into their hair to make it appear grey or white. Draw lines with an eyebrow pencil to suggest wrinkles on their foreheads, at the sides of their mouths, and at outer edges of their eyes. If crepe hair is available, use it to give Franz a short beard.

Dancing dolls will have a more dolllike appearance if you give them brightly rouged cheeks and lips. The color should be put on with a definite outline.

Although painted scenery can add to the visual effect of the play, an effective toyshop can be achieved without it. Narrow tables and shelves of toys can in themselves create a toyshop atmosphere. Players take pride in bringing their own toys for this display. One boy or girl acting as property manager should be responsible for putting toys in place for rehearsal and performance, and for putting them away afterward. After the last performance he sees that all toys are returned to their owners. Each Neighborhood Child may wish to bring the toy he uses or speaks about in the play.

Franz's work table should be small so it does not take up space needed by the players.

Although the play can be produced with little scenery and few stage properties, the players do need hand properties. Such properties can make them feel more at ease with the characters they interpret. Properties give players ideas of what to do with their hands to show personality traits and moods of their characters.

Franz has on his work table the tools and materials for dollmaking. He should use them often. His cap and cape become hand properties when he takes them off right after his entrance. He shows he is in a hurry by the way he tosses them on a chair or table or lets them fall to the floor. Minna uses the same wraps to show her patient helpfulness as she stoops to pick them up, smooths them and lays them carefully on a shelf.

Hilda could play listlessly with a little ball as she enters in the opening scene. The way she tosses or bounces it shows her dejected spirit. Burgomaster has a useful hand property in his purse that holds the gold pieces he later gives to Franz. While Franz gets the dolls Burgomaster may count or toy with the gold. Later, Franz rubs the coins, holds them up to catch the light, and counts them before putting them away. The Messenger could carry a riding whip, which he snaps now and then to give emphasis to his words. Minna has sewing or knitting that she does at appropriate times. Strange Woman might have a staff or walking stick. Later she raises it to suggest a wand when she casts the spell. Franz should show his dislike of the stick, particularly when she waves it on saying, "You will gladly give away all you have."

Neighborhood Children are not apt to carry anything in the opening scene because they want their hands free to carry the toys they expect to receive from Franz. In the end they have hand properties in the toys he gives them.

You can readily see that the play does not need to be presented on a platform. Any place will do that gives the players room to move as suggested in the play and that permits spectators to hear and see them. However, provision should be made to keep players out of sight when they are not acting onstage. If the play is given in a classroom or clubroom players may wait in an adjoining corridor before and after their scenes. When this is not feasible, set up panel screens behind which they can stand before entering and after leaving the playing area.

Listen to the Peace and Goodwill

by Maxine McSweeny

CHARACTERS:

MARSTON, captain of the Martians
SPIES FROM MARS
  MARTHA
  MARGARET
GIDDYAP, driver of Santa's sleigh
    WHOA, loader of toys
SANTA
SEAMSTRESSES
  MRS. RITTENBOTTOM
  MRS. HUGGINS
GUARDS FROM MARS
  MARVIN
  MARTIN

TIME: *Christmas Eve.*

SCENE: *Santa's living room. On the upstage wall is a big map with bold red lines and red dots as big as doorknobs. Beside the map is a sign, "TWO MORE DAYS TIL CHRISTMAS." When this sign is torn off it reveals another sign, "ONE MORE DAY TIL CHRISTMAS."*

At right is an armchair covered by a red drape. Beside it is a table with a book on it. A workbench with a doll on it is at left. An entrance to the workshop is up left. Down right an entrance leads outdoors.

AT RISE: *A clash of cymbals announces the opening of the play and the entrance of the Martian spies, Margaret and Martha. They sneak in right and look cautiously about. Martha then darts behind the workbench. Margaret hides behind the chair. They wear green skull caps from which protrude antennae. Their blouses and short A-line skirts are also green. Small, shiny discs dangle from their belts. On their feet are ballet slippers with green lacings that criscross around their legs almost to their knees.*

When Martians move from one place to another they do not walk. They bend their knees slightly and take slow running steps. As they run they hold their heads and arms motionless. Their hands either hang at their sides or are held palms down against the front of their thighs. Martians do not move their eyes from side to side. When they want to look to the side they turn their heads, usually with a slight jerk. Martians speak with exaggerated distinctness as they sound every syllable and the last letter of every word. Their inflections, however, are natural and never monotonous.

Cymbals sound a second time, and Marston enters. He wears a cap and belt like those of the girls. His shirt and pants are green. The pants are long and gathered close to the ankle by a narrow band of silver paper or ribbon. From it dangle silver discs like those at his belt. Marston Blows a blast on a whistle that hangs on a cord around his neck. Then he calls.

MARSTON: Martha! Martha from Mars!
MARTHA: *(Rises behind the workbench)* Here I am, Captain Marston.
(He nods to her and calls again)

MARSTON: Margaret! Margaret from Mars.
(Margaret rises, crosses in front of him and stands near Martha.)
MARGARET: I am here and ready to work.
MARSTON *(turning to face them):* Margaret and Martha, you were sent here to spy on the earth people. Have you done your job?
MARGARET:
MARTHA: } We have.
MARSTON: What have you learned about this thing they call Christmas?
MARTHA: It's a plot.
MARGARET: A plot to blow up the universe! Every star and planet!
MARSTON: Is that what Christmas means?
MARGARET: Yes. It's a code word.
MARSTON: How do you know?
MARTHA: We watch these people and listen to them. They rush around like mad. The nearer it gets to what they call Christmas, the harder they rush.
MARGARET: Nothing but the end of the universe could make people rush the way they do.
MARTHA: *(goes to sign on wall)* Just look at this. It's the countdown. It shows how many days till blastoff. Today they're so rushed they don't even tear off the page.
(She tears it off to reveal the sign beneath.)
They keep saying, "Hurry! Get ready! It's almost time. Get everything loaded."
MARGARET: Then they get mad. They're mad at everybody.
MARTHA: Everybody except that man in the red suit. He doesn't get mad.
MARGARET: No. But he's the real villain.

MARSTON: He's the reason I sent you here to spy. Just a year ago I saw him out in a little red spaceship with animals in front of it. I knew he was up to something.

MARTHA: And he still is.

MARGARET: Look at this map. (*She leads Marston to the map.*) You see these red dots? They're planets he's going to drop bombs on.

MARSTON: How do you know?

MARTHA: He says things like, "Here's where I'll drop down the chimney."

MARSTON: What's a chimney? What happens when he drops it?

MARTHA: We can't find out. It must be a code word for some new kind of bomb.

MARSTON: (*Overcome by such frightening news he sinks to the arm of a chair.*) Tell me about his little red spaceship. Does he go out in it?

MARGARET: Not since we've been here. But he will tonight. He's had everybody loading things into it all day.

MARSTON: What kind of things?

MARTHA: (*Picks up doll from workbench.*) Things like this dummy — hundreds of them — all dressed in pretty clothes.

MARSTON: (*Goes to inspect doll*) This must be to test the effect of the bomb.

MARGARET: Yes. If it can blow up the dummy it will blow up everything.

MARSTON: You say it's going to happen tonight?

MARTHA: Unless you can stop that little fat man in the red suit — the one they call Santa Claus.

Listen to the Peace and Goodwill

MARSTON: We'll stop him. (*Goes toward outside entrance*) I'll call the guards. We'll take him and his little red spaceship to Mars.
GIDDYAP: (*Calls from workroom*) Get a move on you, Whoa. We have to hurry.
MARGARET: They're coming.
MARTHA (*running toward workbench*): Shall we hide?
MARSTON: No. Come with me. Help guard the spaceship.
(*The three rush outdoors.*)
(*Giddyap enters from workroom. He carries a red bag of toys on his back. Whoa follows dragging a similar bag behind him. They are in a hurry, but Giddyap stops suddenly to look at the map. Whoa bumps into Giddyap, knocks the bag off his back, and scatters toys on the floor.*)
GIDDYAP (*yelling*): Ee-OW! Look what you did.
WHOA: I didn't.
GIDDYAP: You did.
WHOA: I did not.
GIDDYAP: You weren't watching.
WHOA: I was, too.
GIDDYAP (*starting to pick up toys*): You weren't either.
WHOA: I was.
GIDDYAP (*yelling again*): Why don't you help pick up?
WHOA (*picking up one toy and shouting*): I am.
GIDDYAP (*louder than ever*): You're not.
(*Santa enters from outdoors and stands near entrance.*)
SANTA: Boys! You'll frighten the reindeer. Stop quarreling.
GIDDYAP (*all mildness*): I wasn't quarreling.

WHOA (*just as mild as Giddyap*) Yes, you were, Giddyap.
GIDDYAP (*not so mild*): I wasn't.
WHOA (*not mild at all*) You were, too.
GIDDYAP (*yelling*): I was not.

SANTA: Stop it. I'm fed up with the fighting. Everywhere I go—nothing but quarreling. It's almost time to start. (*As he goes outdoors he calls*) I'll be back in a minute.
(*Giddyap and Whoa look accusingly at each other as they pick up toys and stuff them in the bags.*
Mrs. Rittenbottom hurries in from the workshop. She carries a doll.)

MRS. R: Here's another doll. Quick! Get it in. (*She hands doll to Giddyap. Before he can get it in the bag Mrs. Huggins enters from workshop and sees the doll.*)

MRS. H: Mrs. Rittenbottom! That doll's not finished.
MRS. R: Finished or not, it has to go.
MRS. H: It's my work, Mrs. Rittenbottom. I won't let it go until it's done.
MRS. R: Santa can't wait.
MRS. H: (*Grabs doll and shakes it to emphasize her words.*) The dress is only pinned on this doll. (*Holds doll close to her and stands very straight*) No doll of mine is going without its hooks and eyes.
MRS. R: Mrs. Huggins! Your hooks and eyes always come off anyway.
You don't sew them on tight enough.
MRS. H: Oh yes, I do.
MRS. R: No, you don't.
(*They continue "Yes I do" and "No you don't" as Mrs. H. backs toward the*

Listen to the Peace and Goodwill

(*...workroom. Mrs. R follows so closely their faces are only a few inches apart. In the midst of their quarrel Giddyap yells at Whoa.*)

GIDDYAP: Whoa! You're not working. Pick up the toys.

WHOA: (*He is not working, but he says he is*) I AM.

(*Two quarrels at once make a deafening noise. Santa returns.*)

SANTA: Quiet! I can't stand it. (*All four stop and look at Santa. Giddyap runs to him.*)

GIDDYAP: Santa, tell Whoa to help pick up. He made me drop everything.

WHOA (*yelling*): I did not.

GIDDYAP (*also yelling*): You did.

MRS. H (*appearing at workroom entrance*): Santa! Santa!

SANTA: What is it? Boys, be quiet so I can hear Mrs. Huggins.

(*Boys stop yelling but make faces at each other.*)

MRS. H: Santa, Mrs. Rittenbottom won't wait for me to sew the hooks and eyes on this doll dress.

MRS. R (*also at workroom entrance*): There's no time. Besides, her hooks and eyes always fall off.

MRS. H: They don't.

MRS. R: They do.

(*As their quarrel grows louder the boys resume theirs.*)

SANTA: Stop! All of you.

(*The four speak more quietly, but they don't stop.*)

S-T-O-P! STOP! For the love of Christmas peace, stop!

(They stop and look at Santa.) You don't care a thing about Christmas. Nobody does. You just fight. The children fight. The grown people fight. The nations fight. And I'm tired of fighting the whole world. I'm going to stay home tonight.
(For an instant all are too shocked to speak)

MRS. R: You can't stay home. You have to take the toys.

SANTA: Well, I'm just not going to take them this year.

WHOA *(to Mrs. R)*: What does he mean?

MRS. R: He means he's not going.

GIDDYAP: He's got to go. I take care of those reindeer all year just to drive them Christmas Eve. Now I don't get to.
(He throws down the toys he has picked up.) I'm so mad I could chew hollyberries and swallow the thorns.

WHOA: Me, too, Giddyap! *(He kicks a bag of toys across the floor.)*

MRS. R: Now boys, don't give up. Let's see what I can do.
(Boys sit on the workbench. Mrs. R. goes to Santa.)
Santa, think of all the children waiting for you tonight.

SANTA: They're not waiting.

MRS. R: Yes, they are.

SANTA: No, they're not.

MRS. R: They are.

SANTA: They— *(stops as he realizes they are quarrelling.)* Now, you've got me doing

Listen to the Peace and Goodwill 45

it — just like the rest of you. I'm GOING TO STAY HOME. IS THAT CLEAR?
(*The four watch him in silence. He takes a book from the table. The book is not thick, but large enough for the audience to see its title in big letters. The title is PEACE AND GOODWILL.*)
I'm going to read about peace and goodwill. How I'd like to see a little — just a little peace and goodwill.

MRS. R: If you saw some, would you go?
SANTA: I might. I don't think so, but I might.
(*He sits and reads.*)
MRS. R: (*She summons the others to a huddle near the workbench.*)
The only way he'll go is to see some goodwill. Now where can we find some?
MRS. H: Well, certainly not around here.
MRS. R: Now, Mrs. Huggins, this isn't such a bad place.
MRS. H: Oh, the place is all right. It's the people. (*She looks at the boys.*) Aren't you boys ashamed? It's all your fault.
GIDDYAP: It's not. It's yours and Mrs. Rittenbottom's. Your quarrel's worse than ours.
WHOA (*yelling*): It sure is.
MRS. H
MRS. R (*louder*): No, it's not.
GIDDYAP
WHOA (*loudest of all*): Yes, it is.
(*Santa looks over the top of his book at all four of them.*)
SANTA: JUST LISTEN TO THE PEACE. Listen to the peace and goodwill.

	(*Mrs. R. again beckons all into a huddle*). We're not getting any place. We've got to show him some goodwill. How can we do it?
WHOA:	Would it be good will if I helped Giddyap pick up the toys?
MRS. R:	It certainly would. (*Whoa begins to pick up toys and put them in the bags.*)
GIDDYAP:	Oh, Whoa, you shouldn't have to. I spilled them by myself this last time. (*Together the boys pick up toys. Santa lowers his book again and smiles. Mrs. R. notices the smile. She turns to Mrs. H. and speaks in a sugary sweet voice.*)
MRS. R:	Mrs. Huggins, while we wait, why don't you go in and sew on those hooks and eyes? I'll thread needles for you.
MRS. H:	Oh, thank you, Mrs. Rittenbottom. And maybe, you'll show me how you make yours stay on.
MRS. R:	Of course I will. (*They continue their flattering words and sweet tones as they go into the workroom. The boys having picked up all the toys put the bags near the outside entrance. All is quiet. Santa puts his book on the table.*)
SANTA:	Well boys, this sounds more like peace and goodwill.
GIDDYAP:	Now, will you go?
WHOA:	Please, Santa.
SANTA:	Well, I might.

GIDDYAP: *(He runs to the map.)* We have to hurry. *(Points to the third dot from left.)* We ought to be down here right now.

SANTA: Yes, that's just about where we should be. *(Gets up)* Well, let's take a look around the workroom. *(He goes out the workroom entrance. The two boys look at each other as if to say, "Do you think he'll go?" and then follow him out.)*

(The sound of cymbals announces the return of the Martians. Marston peeks in from outdoors. After looking right, then left, he walks cautiously to center. Again he looks right and left. He calls.)

MARSTON: Martin! Marvin! Quick! Come here.

(The two Martian guards enter from outside. They stop near the entrance.)

MARTIN: Here we are.

MARVIN: Your Martian guards stand ready to serve.

MARSTON: There's nobody here. The little man got away.

MARVIN: He couldn't. His spaceship is still here.

MARSTON: Run, Martin. Tell the girls to guard that spaceship. When they hear my whistle they're to run in here. Go.

MARTIN: I'll do it. *(runs off right.)*

MARSTON: Now, Marvin, you know every planet is in danger.

MARVIN: Yes. The girls told me the old man is going to drop chimneys on the planets. They could blow us right into the Milky Way.

MARSTON: *(always on the lookout for danger sees the doll on the workbench.)* Get that dummy. He won't test his bombs on that one.

(Marvin hides the doll under the bench. Martin returns.)

MARTIN: He hasn't gone. The spaceship's there and still loaded. *(Marston goes to entrance to meet Martin and beckons Marvin to join them.)*

MARSTON: Whatever happens, guard this entrance. He'll never get out.

GIDDYAP: *(Entering from workroom he looks in surprise at Martians. He stops just inside the entrance.)* What-what do you want?

MARSTON: We want that little man in the red suit.

GIDDYAP: You mean Santa Claus?

MARSTON: Yes. We won't hurt you. We just want him.

GIDDYAP: *(moving center to get a better look at the Martians)*: What do you want him for?

MARVIN: To take him to Mars.

MARTIN: So he won't blow up the universe.

(As Giddyap looks at them in disbelief, Santa is heard from the workroom.)

SANTA: *(offstage)* Everybody ready? Ho! Ho! Ho!

MARSTON: That's the signal. *(He blows his whistle. Margaret and Martha run in.)* Girls! Help guard the door. Don't let any one out. *(Girls stand near Martin and Marvin.)* *(Whoa enters up left leading Santa and the seamstresses. The three of them repeat Santa's "Ho! Ho! Ho!")*
(Giddyap rushes to protect Santa from the Martians.)

GIDDYAP: Santa! Get back! Go Back!

(Santa steps aside to look at the Martians.)

SANTA: What's going on here?

GIDDYAP:	Run! They're going to kidnap you. *(Santa pushes Giddyap out of his way. Those around him are too surprised to move. The Martians don't move because they want to guard the entrance. For an instant no one moves or speaks as each group looks at the other.)*
SANTA:	Why do you want to kidnap me? *(Marston nods to his guards and spies to stay by the entrance. He steps toward Santa. When the boys and seamstresses see this move they move close behind Santa to protect him from possible danger. Santa speaks again and in a loud voice)* WHY DO YOU WANT TO KIDNAP ME?
MARSTON:	So you won't blow up the universe.
SANTA:	I don't want to blow up the universe.
MARSON:	You plan to drop bombs on the planets this very night. *(Mrs. R. steps forward to confront Marston. When she speaks, everybody listens.)*
MRS. R:	Listen, young man! You in the funny, green cap, what did you say?
MARSTON:	I said we're not going to let this man blow up the universe by dropping chimneys.
MRS. R:	He doesn't drop chimneys.
MARGARET:	*(leaving her post by the door she runs to the map.)* Oh yes, he does. I heard him say, 'I've marked a red dot every place I'll drop down the chimney.'
GIDDYAP:	He doesn't drop chimneys. He drops *down inside* chimneys.
MARTHA:	What is a chimney? Why does he want inside it?

MRS. R: It's just a way to get into houses and leave presents.

MARSTON: We don't have presents where we come from. What are they?

MRS. R: The things you give people because you like them and want to make them happy. (*Santa listens closely but says nothing.*)

MARGARET: Are you trying to make people happy?

MRS. R: Of course. That's what Christmas is for.

MARTHA: Well, why do you rush around so?

MRS. R: To get the presents there on time.

WHOA: We have to get them there by Christmas.

MARSTON: If you're just trying to show people you like them why do you get so mad? (*The five in Santa's group look questioningly at one another.*)

MRS. H: I guess we just try too hard. (*Santa moves toward Marston to take command of the situation.*)

SANTA: Now, that explains us. But what about you? Who are you anyway?

MARSTON: We're from Mars. We saw you last year. You were flying through the night sky in a little red spaceship. I thought you were up to something. I sent spies here to protect the planets.

SANTA: Well, now, I won't hurt your planets. I just want a little peace and goodwill. Come out to my sleigh—what you call my spaceship. I've presents for you—Martians and all the rest. Then we have to get started. We're already late. Now line up. Martians first, seamstresses next, then Giddyap and Whoa. And here we go. HO! HO! HO!

>   (*Everyone, even the Martians, takes up the shout as all go through the outside entrance in the order Santa described.*)
> ALL: HO! HO! HO!
>
>   (*As the last person leaves the stage a clash of cymbals signals the end of the play.*)

[THE END]

SUGGESTIONS FOR THE DIRECTOR

Regarding Rehearsal and Production of *Listen to the Peace and Good Will*

This play is a comedy, almost a farce, so let the actors get all possible fun from rehearsing and presenting it. The play's appeal is primarily to eight- and ten-year-olds. Children a little older or younger will enjoy the play if they like spacemen comic books or television serials. The Martians may be all boys or all girls depending on available players.

Players should rollick through the quarrels and the attemps to kidnap Santa Claus before they memorize lines or movement. This is particularly important for younger children or those without previous acting experience. This play may be the means of drawing into drama activity children who are hard to reach because of their poverty, ghettolike living, or shyness.

First, read the play to the prospective players, or tell them its story. Lead them in a short discussion of quarreling. Stimulate them to think about quarrels with questions like these:

Did you ever quarrel with another child?
How did you start?
Did you get madder as the quarrel continued?

Did you yell?

When did you yell loudest?

How did you show you were getting angrier? (Remember this is a quarrel, not a fight. In a quarrel you do not strike or knock your opponent down.)

How do you show increasing anger with your eyes? Your mouth? Teeth? Hands? Feet?

Do grownups quarrel in the same way children do?

How would their quarrels differ?

Would the Seamstresses' quarrel differ from that of the boys?

After players discuss answers to these questions divide the group of players into pairs. Each pair plans a quarrel to present for the entire group. Give them these instructions to help them plan:

Decide whether you are Seamstresses or Whoa and Giddyap in your quarrel.

Decide how to enter. Do you come in together or separately? One of you does something to cause the other to say, "You did." Plan the cause.

In your quarrel use only the words, "You did." and "I didn't."

Say them no more than four times each.

Plan how the quarrel ends.

Do you leave together or separately?

Allow five minutes for planning. Then each pair presents its quarrel scene for the others.

Next, turn the players' thoughts to the kidnap scene. Tell them that Marston's efforts to capture Santa, and the efforts of Santa's friends to protect him are like a game of Cat and Rat. Organize players for this game. Children stand in a circle and clasp hands. Choose one child for Cat, and another for Rat. Rat stands inside the circle. Outside it stands Cat. They talk:

CAT: I'm Cat.

RAT: I'm Rat.
CAT: I'll catch you.
RAT: No, you won't.
CAT: Yes, I will. And this is how I'll do it.

As Cat says the last line he tries to break through the circle and tag Rat. Those making the circle protect Rat by raising and lowering their hands and standing close together whenever Cat tries to break through. When Cat succeeds he chooses a new Rat, then joins hands with others in the circle. The former Rat becomes Cat, and a new game starts. Two games are enough.

Another activity that should precede actual rehearsal of the play is a talk about the Martians. The script suggests the way they walk, speak, and hold their heads and hands. Draw out the players' ideas about the appearance and manners of the Martians. Ask children how spacemen in comic books and television serials act as distinguished from earth people. It is good for children to recognize your interest in what they know. Relating their knowledge to the play gives them a fine educational activity.

After the discussion let children demonstrate their ideas of how Martians act. They should do this first in one big group, and then in pairs. You should point out some good aspect of each child's efforts. Some of the players' ideas may be so effective you will want to include them in rehearsal and performance. Such recognition increases players' self-confidence and stimulates them to greater effort.

The discussions, the game, and the impromptu acting take place at the first rehearsal. These activities should give players a taste of the thrill of being in a play, and confidence in their ability to act it. The informal activities should also move players forward in their feeling for the play so that rehearsal time can be shortened.

At the end of this first rehearsal, explain to the players

how preparing a play for an audience differs from their informal acting quarrels and playing Martians. To give pleasure to an audience players need to act according to a plan that offers the most exciting things to say and do. Much of this plan is contained in the script. So you assign roles to specific players and give them copies of the script when you begin organized rehearsal.

After the informal activity described above, players are ready to read their lines in the script. Next, you show them where they move from one place to another. In this play the actors will run, dodge, sneak, as well as walk when moving from one part of the stage to another. They practice all of this according to plan so that by performance time players know what to do and where to go as surely as they know what to say. Practice the timing of movements and coordinating them with one another. This should provide fun at rehearsal, and later, fun for an audience.

As players rehearse speeches and movement you should help them keep the spontaneity and enthusiasm of their impromptu acting. In it they expressed something of the character of the people in the play. Help participants build on these initial characterizations. By the fourth rehearsal Giddyap and Whoa should practice with the bag of toys—spilling and picking them up. The Seamstresses begin to work with the doll that causes their quarrel. On the table should be the *Peace and Goodwill* book that Santa reads. A second doll should be in place so Marston can practice hiding it under the bench.

Actors in this play work to create suspense. They need to make the audience wonder what is going to happen. With increasing concern spectators should be asking themselves:

Will the Martians learn that Christmas is not dangerous?
Will Santa relent and deliver the toys?
What will happen if he goes to his sleigh where the Martians wait to capture him?

Listen to the Peace and Goodwill

Will there be a fight between Santa's friends and the Martians?

Will the Martians capture Santa?

Here are some devices players can use to sharpen suspense and keep the audience wondering what will happen.

1. At play's opening Margaret and Martha sneak in slowly as though afraid of making a noise and attracting attention. They stop every few steps and look around to check on their surroundings and to see if they are followed. Suddenly they stop sneaking and dash to hiding places. This sudden change of pace should excite the audience at the very beginning of the play.

2. Martians say "Christmas" so as to veil the word in mystery. Try pausing immediately before and after speaking the word. Say it in a hushed tone that contrasts with the rest of the sentence.

3. Marston shows great fright when Martha tells him a chimney is some kind of bomb. She says the word *bomb* as if she knows it could blow them to bits. This news makes Marston so weak he drops to the arm of the chair. A minute later he recovers and with a mightly show of strength says, "We'll stop him." Before he says it he shows he has conquered his weakness and resolves to act. He says, "We'll stop him" with such determination that the audience shudders with fear of what he is about to do.

4. When the Martians hear Giddyap call from the workroom Martha and Margaret are so frightened they dart back and forth not knowing whether to hide or run away. Marston solves their problem with a quick command, "Come with me. Guard the spaceship!" As they run out they look back to show their fear of being followed.

5. Let the tension ease now and then, only to build up again. Suspense should diminish as Giddyap and Whoa enter the first time. It starts to build with their quarrels until it reaches

another climax when Santa says he will not go. New suspense is then created as the seamstresses plot with Giddyap and Whoa to make Santa relent. From here on suspense grows steadily to the climax of the play. This is on Giddyap's speech, "He doesn't drop chimneys."

6. When Giddyap, Whoa, and the Seamstresses encircle Santa to protect him from Martians, they hold their circle for four or five speeches. Marston tries to break through the circle when he says, "So you can't blow up the universe," and again on the speech, "Yes, you do." As children practice this scene, remind them of the way they acted when they played Cat and Rat. When Marston fails to break the circle he steps back, stands still, and says, "You're dropping bombs tonight." Mrs. Rittenbottom in anger and amazement steps out of the circle and turns on him to say, "Listen, young man." Then the solving of the mystery begins with Giddyap's speech, "He doesn't drop chimneys." Martians drop their warlike attitudes and listen closely for answers to their questions. The suspense is over, and everyone relaxes.

Sound effects can increase suspense as well as help create atmosphere for the play. Note the script instruction for the sound of cymbals at the beginning and conclusion of the play and on the entrance of the Martians. Add this sound effect each time the Martians leave the stage.

Use real cymbals if possible. If you cannot obtain them, substitute other equipment. Let players experiment with sounds they can make with kettles, skillets, lids, rolling pin, and hammer. Children will enjoy trying out sounds. The activity should sharpen their ability to discriminate as to pitch, quality, and volume. Those who participate in these experiments should share in deciding which equipment makes the most suitable sound.

Designate one or two children as sound effects technicians. You may have more children wishing to be in the play than the number of roles it offers. From the extras select the sound technicians. If there are no extra children, assign the responsibilities to Martin and Marvin. Their parts are small, and their time onstage is so short they can assume additional duties.

The technicians work with players at several of the last rehearsals. They need this practice to get the right effect at exatly the right time. Players also need such rehearsal to coordinate their entrances and other movements with sound.

In addition to the cymbals, music can be used with good effect. Immediately following the first clash of cymbals a piano, flute, or violin may accompany the Martians' opening entrance. The music creates atmosphere for sneaking movements, then changes to accompany their dash to hiding places. Similar instrumental music may be heard during all pantomime when there is no speaking. Examples are moments like picking up toys; Santa's sitting down to read; and his entrance with Seamstresses, Giddyap, and Whoa the first time he says, "Ho! Ho! Ho!" Most effective of all will be music at the play's conclusion. It begins as soon as Santa says, "Here we go." The selection should be a merry Christmas carol like "Jingle Bells" or "Santa Claus Is Coming to Town."

As to scenery for this play, the big map provides its background. Stretch a roll of butcher paper at eye level across the back of the stage and draw a map on it. Children should participate in this. Let them look at road maps to get ideas for their drawing. Point out such details as the legend that gives the key to different kinds of roads and the scale of miles. Many children should draw small sketches of the way they think the big map should look. They look at these sketches and discuss them with you. Some of your players may be skilfull enough to execute the big map. They may want to print on it the names of cities and towns near them, particularly their own.

Costumes are another consideration. The script suggests what the Martians wear. You may substitute your own ideas or those of the players. For instance, jumpsuits with attached, fitted hoods would be just as effective as the costumes described in the script.

Seamstresses wear long dresses with fitted bodices and gathered skirts. Add aprons—either short, fancy ones or plain, long ones. Their costumes should include such sewing accessories as pincushions attached to bands around their wrists, scissors hanging from tapes at their waists, even a few pins near the shoulders of their bodices.

Giddyap and Whoa will look like Santa's drivers if they wear red T shirts or sweaters, long dark trousers, and pointed red caps. The trousers may be cords, jeans, or other type of dark work pants. These boys might also wear boots into which they tuck the ends of the trousers.

Santa should have the familiar long, white beard, but no mask. With him in traditional Santa Claus suit, every player is dressed for performance.

The Transfiguration of the Gifts

by Frances Cavanah

CHARACTERS:

MARY, Mother of Jesus

THE THREE WISE MEN

THE RAGGED BOY

THE STURDY BOY

THE GIRL OF UNSELFISH SPIRIT

THE LITTLEST CHILD

THE CHRISTMAS ANGEL

THE ANGEL CHOIR

SCENE: *Interior of the stable at Bethlehem. There is an exit at left center. The manger, with a stool beside it, is down right.*
Before the curtains* open and without announcement the

---

*See Suggestions for the Director at the end of the play for a way to produce the play without curtains.

Angel Choir sings one verse of "O Holy Night" or one verse of "Hark the Herald Angels Sing." Curtains then open to disclose Mary seated by the manger. She looks tenderly at the Christ Babe in the manger. The Angels stand upstage in a wide semicircle. The Christmas Angel stands at extreme left. Angel Choir sings one verse of "O Little Town of Bethlehem." As the Angels sing they gather around Mary. Each in turn pauses to look at the Babe. At the end of the song the Angels again take their position in a semicircle. The Christmas Angel kneels by the manger.
Sturdy Boy peeps shyly in the left doorway. The other children look over his shoulder.

STURDY BOY: May we see the Christ Babe?
CHRISTMAS ANGEL (*hastening to them*): Not yet.
RAGGED BOY (*disappointed*): Oh, we've come so far.
LITTLEST
 CHILD: And I'm so tired, Angel.
CHRISTMAS ANGEL (*smiling at them*): Be quiet, children. Three Kings are here.
LITTLEST CHILD (*awestruck*): Oh!
RAGGED BOY (*disappointed*): Oh!
GIRL OF UNSELFISH SPIRIT (*excited*): Are real kings coming here?
CHRISTMAS
 ANGEL: Yes, three wise men. They come to bring gifts.
RAGGED BOY (*eagerly*): We have gifts, too.
CHRISTMAS
 ANGEL: You may give them to the Babe in a few minutes, child.
STURDY BOY: We heard that the Christ Child wore a crown.

The Transfiguration of the Gifts

GIRL OF UNSELFISH SPIRIT: Not the kind King Herod wears, but a crown of light.

CHRISTMAS ANGEL: Yes, it is called his halo. You may see it in a little while, but you must wait now. (*Smiling at them, she closes the door just as the Three Wise Men enter from the rear of the audience. They are singing "We Three Kings of the Orient Are," and are joined by the Angel Choir. They move in dignified procession to the stage where they kneel in adoration before the manger and present their gifts. They resume their song and leave as they came, through the auditorium.*
As soon as the Wise Men disappear through the rear door of the auditorium, the children again peek in the doorway at left.)

RAGGED BOY: May we see the Christ Babe now?

LITTLEST CHILD: We have such pretty gifts.

CHRISTMAS ANGEL: Yes. Come children, but remember this is sacred ground.
(*Children enter, proudly bearing their offerings but stop in confusion when they see the costly presents left by the Wise Men. They seem ready to cry.*)

CHRISTMAS ANGEL: Come, the Christ Babe waits for you.

STURDY BOY: Oh, no, we couldn't now.
CHRISTMAS ANGEL (*gently*): But why?
GIRL OF UNSELFISH SPIRIT (*pitifully holding out the little cotton coverlet she carries*): Our gifts, bright Angel.
LITTLEST CHILD (*disappointed as she looks at the wilted field lily in her hand*): And we thought they were so pretty.
CHRISTMAS ANGEL: They are.
STURDY BOY: No, no! Look at the presents the Wise Men left. They are for a king. We brought ours to a baby in a manger.
CHRISTMAS ANGEL: The King lies in the manger, children. Don't be afraid to take your gifts to Him. Your gifts are pretty.
STURDY BOY: No, no!
CHRISTMAS ANGEL (*turning to Mary*): Mother of Jesus, I'm afraid they don't understand.
MARY (*coaxingly*): Come children. I know your gifts are lovely. (*They shake their heads.*) Oh, come! (*Sturdy Boy, Girl of Unselfish Spirit, and the Littlest Child draw closer to her, fascinated by her voice and smile. They kneel in adoration. In pantomime the Christmas Angel vainly tries to persuade Ragged Boy to approach the manger.*)
MARY: Now, I must see your offerings. (*The children glance with apprehension at the gold and frankincense left by the Wise Men.*) The soul of those gifts is no more beautiful than the soul of yours.
GIRL OF UNSELFISH SPIRIT (*surprised*): Do gifts have souls?

MARY:	The kind gifts do. And sometimes the humblest gift has the prettiest soul.
STURDY BOY:	Mother of Jesus, our presents are very poor. Is that what "humble" means?
MARY:	Yes, Sturdy Boy. (*Coaxingly*) Let me see what you have brought.
STURDY BOY:	Only a little hay. I heard that the innkeeper would not give the Babe a bed. I knew if he had to sleep in the manger, the hay would make it softer. The straw has stickers sometimes. I know because I sleep on it at home.
MARY (*helping him place the hay carefully under the Babe*):	Tuck the hay carefully. (*After the hay is in place she looks joyfully at him.*) I *thought* your gift would be beautiful.
STURDY BOY (*bashfully*):	But it was only hay.
MARY:	Yes, but it made a soft bed for the Babe. This is the way He transfigures all the gifts that come to him.
STURDY BOY (*gaining confidence*):	Doesn't it smell sweet? For a baby I think it smells better than myrrh.
MARY (*sniffing it*):	Very sweet. (*To Girl of Unselfish Spirit*) And your present, dear child?
GIRL OF UNSELFISH SPIRIT: (*handing her a coverlet*):	My coverlet. It isn't made of silk as a baby king's should be, but it is the only one I have.
MARY:	The only one? What will you do when the cold wind creeps into your bed at night?
GIRL OF UNSELFISH SPIRIT: (*cheerfully as she clutches her shawl to her more closely*):	Oh, I'll wrap up in my shawl. The wind won't get me.

MARY: (*tucking coverlet about the Babe*): Do you know how beautiful your offering is?

GIRL OF UNSELFISH SPIRIT: But it isn't silk or even wool. It's only a cotton coverlet.

MARY: Yes, but it made the Christ Babe warm. Again, a gift has been transfigured. Now, Littlest Child, show us what you brought.

LITTLEST CHILD: (*holding a wilted lily behind her back, she is nearly sobbing*): I picked a field lily, but—it wilted on the way. It—it was so pretty. I know the Christ Babe would have liked it.

MARY: (*gently*): Let me see it.

LITTLEST CHILD: (*protesting*): But, Mother of Jesus, it is wilted.

MARY: (*insisting*): Give it to me, little one.
(*The faded field lily droops pitifully as Littlest Child holds it out.*)

LITTLEST CHILD: See.

MARY: Put it in the manger. (*The child puts the drooping lily in the manger. Then she looks up and smiles. Mary lifts from the manger a fresh and shining lily that has been concealed there. The child is transfixed by wonder.*)

LITTLEST CHILD: But—but it was wilted.

MARY (*laying the lily in the manger again*) The Christ Babe can revive even a wilted flower when it is given to Him in a spirit of love.

STURDY BOY (*speaking so the Ragged Boy cannot hear*):

The Transfiguration of the Gifts

	The Ragged Boy came with us, but he is afraid to show his gift.
MARY:	Where is he now?
STURDY BOY:	By the door.
MARY (*seeing him for the first time*):	Poor Little Ragged Boy, won't you come to me? (*When he remains silent*) Don't you want to see the Christ Babe?
RAGGED BOY:	Oh, yes.
MARY:	Then, come.
	(*The Christmas Angel takes him by the hand and guides his reluctant steps toward the manger. Mary puts her arm around him and draws him toward the manger.*)
RAGGED BOY (*holding something in the closed fist he has hastily placed behind him*):	But I have no gift.
MARY:	No gift?
RAGGED BOY (*looking longingly at the manger*):	None good enough for Him.
MARY (*drawing his hand into her lap*):	Let me see, child. The gifts of your friends were humble. Yet some hay made the Babe a soft bed; a cotton cover made Him warm; and a wilted lily bloomed again. It will be the same with yours.
RAGGED BOY:	It couldn't be, Mother of Jesus. I have only a few stones. I tried to polish them, but they are only pebbles.
GIRL OF UNSELFISH SPIRIT:	But see how he cut his foot in looking for them. He had to limp here all the way.
MARY:	Yet he says they are unworthy.

RAGGED BOY: They are only pebbles.
MARY: Look! The Christ Babe is holding out his little hand for them. Open quickly.

(The children crowd around him eagerly as he timidly places the stones in the manger. Then he gives a gasp of astonishment, as do the other children. Mary lifts from the manger a short string of pearls previously placed there. She holds them up for all to see.)

STURDY BOY (*awed*): Pearls!
GIRL OF UNSELFISH SPIRIT (*her voice shaking*): The lovely pearls!
LITTLEST CHILD: (*gleefully*): Look how they shine!
MARY: (*exultantly*): Still another gift transfigured!

(As the Ragged Boy kneels to present his offering a white light falls across his face. The other children look on in awe. While the Angel Choir sings "Joy to the World," the stage is gradually darkened until, by the end of the song, it is in blackness.

Choir sings only the first verse of the song, and then repeats it. A few spectators should be told in advance that the audience should join the choir in singing the repeat.)

THE END

SUGGESTIONS FOR THE DIRECTOR

Regarding Rehearsal and Production of *The Transfiguration of the Gifts*

Of all the plays in this book this one is easiest to rehearse and produce. Six- to eight-year-olds have given it for limited numbers of spectators. Ten- and twelve-year-olds have done it for larger audiences. Both age groups have been thrilled with the pleasure their performances gave to those who watched.

Both age groups had the support of well-trained singers. The play is short—a nativity scene brought to life and a dramatic setting for the singing of carols. Singing is essential to the production, and rehearsal of the singers is important. If the play is presented by a church group the regular church choir may sing the carols. Such experienced singers add greatly to the effectiveness of a performance. Singers may be children, teenagers, or adults. There should be at least ten singers, and twenty are better. Help them realize that their skillful performance is as necessary as that of the players to a good production. If singers are inexperienced, choose the easiest of Christmas carols. Insist on practice until they sing so well the songs can give pleasure to listeners. There may be a choir director who will take responsibility for the singing. Singers practice by themselves until the last two or three rehearsals, when they work with the players.

A good way to start rehearsal of the players is to tell them the story of the play and let them act it in their own words before they read the script. This lets them act the characters before they worry about reading or learning lines. It can move them to act in a way natural to children and to effect a more sincere and convincing performance. Impromptu acting of the play's story usually shortens the rehearsal time that must be devoted to characterization.

This story is ideal for children's impromptu acting. Most of them have some familiarity with its background and some of the characters. The plot is so simple and develops so logically it is easy for children to remember. What happens to the players is close to children's own experience, and so it is easy for them to portray.

After you tell the story, lead the players in a discussion of it. This prepares them for acting. Talk about the people in the play. Ask questions, and encourage children to answer them informally. To help players recall the steps of the plot and consider the feelings of its characters, try these questions:

What people are there in the stable when the story starts?
What is Mary doing? How does she feel about the Babe in the Manger?
Does the Christmas Angel admire Him?
What children peek from the entrance? Are they excited?
Are they eager to bring their gifts to the Babe?
What causes them to be ashamed of their gifts?
Why do the Three Kings come?
What do they bring?
Do they feel they are in a holy place? How do they show this feeling?
How can they show they are kings by the way they walk, carry their gifts, and present them?

Discussion of answers to these questions should prepare children to interpret the characters and action of the opening scene. Before they begin to act it help them plan their playing area. Ask:

Where shall we have the manger?
Where does Mary sit?
Where are the children when they peek in?
Where do the Three Kings enter?
Do they need to walk a long way so they can show how kingly they are?

Do the Kings leave in the direction from which they entered?

Decisions regarding these questions should be made quickly so children can begin to act. Assign parts, clap your hands as a signal to start, and let players act the opening scene.

Then, discuss the middle of the story. Stimulate children's thinking and their discussion with these questions:

How do children in the play feel when they see the Kings' gifts?
How do they show they are ashamed of their own gifts?
Who encourages them to present their gifts?
What do the first two presents do for the Babe?
What happens when the last two gifts are placed in the Manger?
Is Mary happy to see the children's shame turn to pride and joy?
Do they grow more excited as each gift is transfigured?
Which gift causes the greatest excitement?
Is this the most exciting moment of the entire story?
What can the players do to make it so?
How does the story end?

After discussing these topics the players act the middle and end of the story. You may want to divide it into two scenes. Act first the presentation of gifts by the first two children. Then discuss the last two presentations immediately before they are enacted.

This impromptu acting helps you select players for specific roles in the performance. You can note which children have physical characteristics suited to various roles. An obvious example is that Mary, Christmas Angel, and the Three Kings should be taller than the players who portray the four children. You want actors who have the right voice quality for their roles. In the session of playing the story you can judge this as well as their capacity to enact specific roles.

As you cast the play you may find that those who act the four children want conventional names instead of such script designations as "The Littlest Child." If they do, let them choose their desired names. List some appropriate biblical names like Joel, Amos, Peter, Rachel, Elizabeth, and Anna. From such a list players select their favorites.

After assigning roles you distribute the scripts. The lines of the play are easy to learn, even easier after players have acted the story. But the movement of players about the stage in this play demands particular attention. At most times the position of players and their grouping should remind one of a Christmas card scene or of nativity pictures by the master artists. Refer to both these sources when you are planning players' locations on the stage and their movement about it.

Group the players so they are not all huddled in one part of the stage. The opening scene suggests groups that make an interesting and dramatic picture. Mary is near the manger at right. Just inside the entrance at left are the four children with the Christmas Angel nearby. The Three Kings entering make up a third group. If possible, plan their entrance down an aisle through the audience. Their procession down an aisle gives them space enough to show their kingliness, distinguishes them from other characters, and fills the time the choir requires to sing a stanza or two of "We Three Kings."

Groupings change frequently during the play. The Christmas Angel moves from the entrance to a place above* and right of the manger. She does this to show the Three Kings where to place their gifts. Then she moves left to center and watches them. The Three Kings walk in stately procession above the manger to the place indicated by the Christmas Angel. There they turn toward the manger, extend their hands holding gifts in gestures of presentation and adoration. Then they put down

*The stage term *above* means farther away from the audience. *Down* or *below* means closer to the audience.

the gifts, and one by one, kneel an instant beside the manger before they return down the aisle. It is important that they face the audience as well as the manger when they present their gifts, and again, when they kneel in adoration. To accomplish this they must at both times be above the manger, and not in front of it. Productions have been marred when adoring characters, whether kings or children, knelt below the manger with their backs to the audience. There are times when a player turns his back toward the audience, particularly if he wants to focus attention on another player. But at the moment of adoration the one who worships is the important character, and the audience wants to see his face. Such considerations make it important for you to rehearse players until they know their position and movement during the entire play.

The singing of "We Three Kings" continues throughout the entrance of the Three Kings, their time onstage, and until they disappear beyond the audience after their return procession up the aisle. As they leave, the Christmas Angel returns to the children at left. Their group changes continually as one by one the children approach the manger and become part of the group there. Here again, at the moment each makes his presentation he should be above the manger so he can face the audience while facing the manger.

By the time three children are in the manger group it changes. Just before Sturdy Boy says, "Doesn't it smell sweet?" he sniffs the hay. Then he crosses in front of the manger and stands above and to the right of Mary. As he moves he looks at the Three Kings' gifts and says with relief, "For a baby, I think it smells better than myrrh." He stands admiring the Kings' gifts but also pleased with his own.

Then he watches as Girl of Unselfish Spirit offers her blanket. She responds to Mary's praise of the blanket with the amazed words, "But it isn't silk, or even wool." She is so impressed with the comfort her gift gave that she walks down left to think about the wonder of it all and look with awe at her surroundings. As she walks she muses, "It's only a cotton coverlet."

When Mary turns to Littlest Child, then Sturdy Boy and Girl of Unselfish Spirit from their new locations look intently toward the manger. After Littlest Child's wilted lily blooms fresh, and all have shown their joy in it, Sturdy Boy looks toward the entrance and sees Ragged Boy there. At the same time Littlest Child sits on the floor in front of the Manger.

Thus she makes room for Ragged Boy to have that important place above the Manger. Sturdy Boy tiptoes to Mary and stands a little above her so the audience sees his face as he talks. It can also see Mary's face since she looks toward the audience as she listens. Her face shows her sympathy for Ragged Boy. Turning left she signals Christmas Angel to bring Ragged Boy to her. He in his turn stands above the manger so the audience can see his face as he looks toward the manger and Mary. The most exciting moment of the play occurs when his shame turns to joy at the sight of the pearls. His face shows both feelings, first the shame and shyness, and next, the joy. He must face the audience at this moment so it can see the change of feeling in his face.

At the instant Mary lifts the pearls all four children gasp in amazement. Remember that the audience does not see the transfiguration of gifts in the manger. The audience sees only how the characters feel about the transfiguration so players must show this with great vividness. Sturdy Boy takes a quick step or two down right to get a better look. Girl of Unselfish Spirit and Christmas Angel draw close to each other at left. They move together as though overcome with the wonder of the miracle. Littlest Child reaches out to grasp the hand of Ragged Boy. He, of course, is so transfixed with happiness that his face is radiant, and he neither speaks nor moves.

After you give players direction for their movement they walk through it two or three times. Then they memorize it as they memorize their speeches. At each rehearsal they practice both lines and movement and go through timing and location exactly as planned for performance.

Emphasize to players that an audience enjoys a performance as much through what it sees as what it hears. To help players appreciate the importance of posture and location, bring nativity pictures for them to study. Point out the various ways the Three Kings stand, carry their gifts, and kneel in adoration in the different pictures. Illustrations showing shepherds at the manger suggest appropriate positions for the four children. Pictures of Madonna and Child help Mary make her role alive and reverent. From the many pictures of angels with their song of peace and good will, the Christmas Angel will receive inspiration and practical suggestions for positions of head, hands, and body. Positions should not be static as in a picture. They should be alive, moving, and filled with joy and adoration. The Angel Choir members will get ideas from the same sources. Their occasional movements should not distract attention from the play.

The choir fulfills several functions in the play. First, of course, is its singing. It also constitutes the background scenery as it stands in a semicircle across the back of the stage. It may also provide a front curtain that conceals the entrance of players at the beginning, and their exit after the play is concluded. To accomplish this, put the manger, the only stage property, in place long before spectators arrive. The performance begins with the choir entering and singing its opening carol. This entrance may be either through the audience or from the side of the stage. As they sing, the choir members move until they stand close together across the front of the stage. Mary then enters behind the choir, unseen by the audience, and takes her place by the Manger. Christmas Angel enters left and stands just inside the entrance. The choir also hides her entrance. As the choir sings the final stanza the singers turn, walk past the Manger, nod or smile or extend their hands as they pass it, and stand in a semicircle across the back of the stage. They should make a beautiful picture as well as a melodious sound.

For costumes almost any style of traditional choir robe is suitable. Colors should be white, pastel, or deep. Wings are rarely worth the trouble they cause both maker and wearer. If each angel wears a halo the wings are not apt to be missed. To make a halo, cut a circle of cardboard that fits securely over the head about halfway between forehead and crown of the head in front, and at the top of the neck in back. The rim of the circle should be two to three inches wide in front and taper along the sides to no more than an inch in back. Shorter singers should have narrower halos. The halo should be cut either from gold cardboard or painted gold after it is cut.

Give some consideration to Angels' feet. Ideal are white or gold ballet slippers. If these cannot be obtained have singers wear white socks and no shoes. Roll the socks down to form a low ridge on the ankle.

The Three Kings should wear socks rolled down in the same way, but theirs should be of dark color. Mary's feet should be covered in the same way with white socks. Although her feet may never show they will be in keeping with her costume if they do.

The four children should have bare feet. Be sure the stage floor is clean for the performance. Otherwise the soles of their feet will be discolored and obvious as children kneel at the Manger.

Children's costumes are simple, smocklike garments. Cut one like a pillow case. Make it wide enough to fit loosely around the player's body. Leave an opening in the seam at the end of the pillow case just long enough to go over the child's head. This opening is the neck of the garment. For armholes leave openings in both side seams seven or eight inches down from the sewed end. Tie a cord or narrow strip of cloth around the waist for a girdle. The smocks vary in length from mid-thigh on the boys to just above the knee on the girls. Costumes are made of coarse cotton or flannel fabric in dark colors. As to fabric design, stripes are appropriate. So is an indeterminate, unpatterned mixture of colors woven closely together.

The Three Kings need two garments each, one worn over the other. The undergarment is full length with kimono sleeves and a plain round neck. The only seams are the long side seams that reach from the lower end of the sleeve to underarm and continue down to the hem of the garment. This is worn with a wide cloth girdle of contrasting color or of metallic gold cloth. The outer garment is cut like the children's smocks except that it is longer, almost as long as the undergarment. In addition to openings for arms and neck this outer robe is open all the way down the front so it reveals a garment beneath.

Kings' costumes should be of rich fabric and in rich colors. Suitable fabrics are medium-weight drapery cloth, cotton velour, cotton satin, nylon taffeta or satin, velvet, or velveteen. Like the children's fabric, appropriate fabric design for the Kings includes bright stripes of varying widths, many-colored threads woven in unpatterned mixture, and Paisley pattern.

The simplest headgear for the Three Kings is composed of a gold crown worn over a head drape that reaches from the forehead in front to a place between waist and hem in back. Crowns are made of gold foil with cardboard backing. You may wish to add some gumdrop jewels.

Mary and Christmas Angel will be attractively costumed in nylon robes cut like the Three Kings' underrobes and worn with a narrow girdle. Christmas Angel wears a halo. She might also have tiny, gold paper wings that show above her shoulders. You may wish to costume her in red and gold, or white and silver to suggest Christmas. Almost any color that is not drab or garish will be effective. She might even be in the same color as some or all of the choir members.

Traditional colors for Mary are white and medium blue, but almost any soft color is suitable. She wears a head drape that hangs over her shoulders and at least halfway down her back. It may be held in place by a halo, a cord, or it may hang loose. For further ideas about costumes refer to Christmas card pictures and religious paintings by great artists.

The Least of These

By Ella Wilson and Anna Field

(From "Where Love Is, There God Is Also" by Leo Tolstoi)

CHARACTERS:

MARTIN, a shoemaker
STEPHEN, a street cleaner
CATHERINE, a poor woman
ELSBETH, her little girl
PETER, a small boy
LENORA, his sister
MARYA, an apple vendor
NICHOL, a street boy
KALEND SINGERS

SCENE: *A poorly furnished room in which Martin lives and works. A fireplace is down left. Over the fireplace hangs a religious picture. At left center is a peasant table with a small bench on the left side of it. Close to the table on its right side is a stool. An entrance leading outdoors is right center. Up right, just above the entrance is a small window that looks on the street. An entrance leading to a hall is up left. Up center is a cupboard containing a few brightly colored dishes.*

AT RISE: *A loud thump is heard as if something bumped against the outer door. Martin enters up left, crosses, and looks out the window. Seeing nothing he crosses to the table and picks up a shoe that needs repairing. He looks again at the window as if expecting someone. It seems hard for him to keep his mind on what he is doing as he changes from one thing to another.*

MARTIN: I'll have to put my tea to steep before I start to work.
(*Goes to cupboard, looks in the cannister and finds it almost empty.*)
(*Putting tea to steep in kettle which he hangs on a hook over the fireplace.*) I haven't much tea. It'll soon be time to buy more.
(*As he looks again toward the window he notices some greens on the table.*) I guess I'll put up my Christmas greens. (*Hanging them over fireplace*) Too bad I haven't a wreath to put around my picture.
(*The thumping noise is heard again. Martin hurries to window. He then speaks with both surprise and relief.*) Oh, it's Stephen. He's clearing away the snow from the steps. Poor Stephen! He's getting old. He has scarcely strength to work. He needs a cup of hot tea. (*Opens door and calls*) Stephen!

STEPHEN (*outside*): What is it?

MARTIN: Come in and warm yourself. You're a bit chilled, aren't you?

STEPHEN (*entering*): Yes, my bones ache. (*He scrapes snow from his shoes.*)

The Least of These

MARTIN: Oh, don't bother to wipe off your shoes. Sit down and have a cup of tea. (*Pours a mug of tea, and giving it to Stephen, starts mending the shoe on table.*)

STEPHEN: Thank you. Ever since I've been cleaning the snow on this street the neighbors have told me how kind you are.

MARTIN: That amounts to nothing. Come on, have a bit more tea.

STEPHEN: My, but it's cold today! The snow seems to be extra hard to clean off the streets.

MARTIN: I should think it would. We had such a heavy frost last night.
(*Looks out window.*)

STEPHEN: Are you expecting anyone?

MARTIN: Am I expecting anyone? Well, I hardly know. Yesterday I was reading about Christ, how He suffered and how He came to earth. "Suppose," I thought, "He came to one like me; would I receive Him at all?" And as I was thinking, I heard a voice say, "Martin, Martin, look tomorrow into the street. I am coming." I thought it was the Christ. Now, do you really think I shall see the Christ?

STEPHEN: Well, strange things happen on Christmas Eve. The Wise Men saw the stars, and the Shepherds saw the Angels.

MARTIN: That is so. But come, have a bit more tea.

STEPHEN: No, thank you. This has strengthened and refreshed me, and I must go back to work.

MARTIN: Come again. I'm glad to have company. Good-bye.

STEPHEN: Good-bye (*He goes out, and the sound of his shovel is heard again, but getting farther away and then ceasing. Martin goes back to his work. He hears a child crying outside.*)

ELSBETH (*outside*): I'm so cold, so cold.

(*Martin hurries to door and opens it. Elsbeth and her mother, Catherine, stand just outside as if seeking a moment's shelter from the wind.*)

MARTIN: Come and get warm. Don't stand there in the cold. Come in and warm yourselves. (*They enter hesitantly.*) Sit down by the fire. Don't cry. Here, have a little tea.

CATHERINE: Thank you. (*Tries to quiet Elsbeth.*)

MARTIN (*gently*): Stop crying, little girl (*He gets bread from the cupboard*) Here's some bread for you.

CATHERINE: This tastes so good. It is the first food we've had today. I can get no work. I'm a soldier's wife. They took him off to war months ago, and I've not heard from him. I've spent all I had for food. Our landlady has pity and gives us shelter. But for that I don't know how we should live through it all.

(*The child runs and stands by Martin.*)

MARTIN: Have you no warm clothes?

CATHERINE: Ah, kind friend, this is indeed a time for warm clothes. I pawned my last shawl to get money for food.

MARTIN (*picking up his coat and giving it to Catherine*): Here, take this. It is shabby, but it will keep the little girl warm.

CATHERINE: Oh! Christ reward your kind heart. He

must have sent me by your window.
(Martin frequently looks out window.)

ELSBETH: What are you looking out the window for, sir?

MARTIN: I heard a voice in my dreams telling me that the Christ would visit me today.

ELSBETH: Then you must put a candle in the window.

MARTIN: Surely we must. It is so dark the Christ could hardly find the way without a little light.

ELSBETH: May I put it in the window?

MARTIN (*lighting candle*): Yes

ELSBETH (*putting it in window*): Oh, it looks so pretty.

CATHERINE (*putting coat around child*): Here, this will keep you warm.

ELSBETH: Oh Mother, that feels good!

CATHERINE: Maybe I can get some work today.

MARTIN: Here my good woman, take this and redeem your shawl. (*Hands her money from his purse*)

CATHERINE: Oh, is this for me? Thank you.

ELSBETH: I hope the Christ-child will see your candle.

MARTIN: Thank you, child. Good-bye and good luck.

(Catherine and Elsbeth leave. Martin picks up the shoe he is repairing. There comes a loud hammering at the door. Martin hurries to open it. A soldier stands there. He strides in, laughing at Martin's startled face.)

SOLDIER: Here, shoemaker, fasten this strap for me, will you, and be quick about it. I'm in a hurry! I'm off to the great dinner yonder. Tra-la-la, and I'm cold. Haven't you any-

thing to drink? Come, man, bring it out.
(*Soldier walks around the room, stamping and clapping his hands.*)

MARTIN: I have just what you want—some nice hot tea.

SOLDIER: Tea! Is that all you have to give me?

MARTIN: I'm sorry I have nothing more, but there's nothing better to warm you on a cold day. I gave some to Stephen, and he said it made him feel strong again.
(*Hands cup of tea to Soldier.*)

SOLDIER: (*Starts to drink and then looks at Martin*) Here, you have none for yourself. Take this. I'm not so cold as I was.

MARTIN: No, no, you drink that. I'm here in the house all day, and you have to go out in the cold. You drink it.

SOLDIER: Well, you're a strange one. But here, we're wasting time. Am I to have this strap fixed? I'm in a hurry.

MARTIN: Yes, yes. Sit down and I'll have it done for you in no time.
(*Martin hurries about getting his needle and thread ready. He pulls up a stool for the soldier.*)

SOLDIER: What! On this stool? What will you do?

MARTIN: I'll work here on the floor. See, you need only unfasten the top of your boot. You need not bother to take it off. That will save time. I need a piece of leather just so long. This is what I need.

SOLDIER: My, you have a large house! And the light—it even hurts my eyes. That candle now—I'll have to put it out. (*Draws his sword to snuff the candle.*)

MARTIN: Oh, sir, don't! Please don't do that! It's the candle to light the Christ-child. (*Continues to work on the boot.*) A little girl put it there. I must keep it lighted.

SOLDIER: To light the Christ-child? Do you believe in such nonsense?

MARTIN: Oh, that isn't nonsense. You see I had a dream; that is, I suppose it was a dream. I heard a voice say, "Martin, Martin, look tomorrow into the street. I am coming." I thought it was the Christ, and I have watched all day, and no one has come but old Stephen and the poor woman with her child. But then it is foolish to expect it. The Christ would hardly find my small door when there are so many waiting for him. (*Standing up*) There, that's finished as good as new. And it wasn't long, was it?

SOLDIER: And very well done, too. Good-bye.
(*Puts a coin in Martin's hand.*)

MARTIN (*looking at coin*): Why, that's far too much. I wasn't five minutes at the whole job. Here, here. (*Hands back a smaller coin.*) And a Merry Christmas to you.

SOLDIER: To you, too, sir.
(*Soldier goes out, then comes back and hesitates.*) Long ago my mother used to put a candle in the window. I used to believe that the Christ-child would come. That was long ago. If He does come, He would come here. You would treat Him right.
(*Soldier leaves, and Martin goes back to his work. Suddenly there are noises as of stomping feet, a knocking, and before*

Martin can move Peter comes in dragging a yule log, and Lenore enters carrying a bowl of wheat.)

PETER: Good evening, Martin. See what we've brought you.

MARTIN: Fine! Fine! Just what I wanted for my Christmas fire. I've been wondering where I could get such a log. I'm so busy I can't find one myself.

(*Peter puts log near fireplace.*)

PETER (*taking handful of wheat from Lenore's bowl and throwing it over log*): Here's my handful of wheat for luck this New Year.

MARTIN: Why not give me a turn? (*Reaches into bowl and touches a chip. Stops and looks in.*) What is this I see?

LENORE: That is the first chip that came from the Christmas tree. I saved it because the tree fell to the east, where the star was.

PETER: When you use our log tomorrow, you must count every spark, for we wish you to have as many customers as there are sparks from this log.

MARTIN: Many thanks for your good wishes.

PETER: Good-bye.

LENORE: Good-bye, and Merry Christmas. (*They leave.*)

MARTIN (*returns again to his work*): I'm afraid I'll never get this shoe finished.

(*He hears sounds of a quarrel outside, and he looks out window.*)

NICHOL (*screaming*): I didn't take it. I didn't take it.

MARYA: You did, you did, you little thief.

(*Martin opens the door. Marya with a*

The Least of These

basket on her arm enters dragging along a boy.) Give me back my apple, I say. (*She hangs on to the boy, who tries to get away.*) I put my basket down to rest my arm, and this dirty little boy took my apples. (*Shakes boy.*)

MARTIN: Let him go, little mother. For the sake of the Christmas Child, let him go. He is not a bad boy. Forgive him.

MARYA: I'll forgive him so he shan't forget the taste of fresh birch rods. I mean to take the rascal to the police station.

MARTIN (*to boy*): Beg the little mother's pardon, and don't do such things any more, I saw you take the apples. (*Hands an apple to the boy and a coin to Marya.*)

MARYA: You will ruin them in that way — the blackguards. If I had the rewarding of him, he should not be able to sit down for a week.

MARTIN: That is our way of looking at things, but it is not God's way. He bade us forgive everyone.

MARYA: But he did steal my apples.

MARTIN: True, but he never will again. You don't want him to spend his Christmas in prison, do you?

MARYA: I never thought of that. Besides, I have boys of my own, and boys are thoughtless. (*Starts to pick up her basket. Nichol reaches for it.*)

NICHOL: Let me take it, little mother; it's on my way home.

MARYA: Well, there's some good in you, after all. (*Nichol takes basket, and they go off together. Martin hears the jingle of bells, and the Kalend Singers are heard singing outside.)*

MARTIN: Here come the Kalend Singers.

(Singers enter. They carry wands from the ends of which hang many colored ribbons and small Christmas bells. They sing and dance. In conclusion they all shout, "Hi!" and troop out. The last singer to leave tears a ribbon from her wand and gives it to Martin.)

SINGER: Here, have a ribbon for good luck.

MARTIN: Thank you. Thank you for your music and your dance.

(With exchange of "Merry Christmas!" "Merry Christmas!" Singers are gone. Their music dies in the distance, and Martin goes back to the table to work. The door bursts open. Judith flies in. She begins to talk rapidly, gesticulating wildly. Martin starts up in surprise.)

JUDITH: Oh, sir, they're chasing me, and throwing stones! Don't let them come in! I'm afraid! I'm afraid! I ran as fast as I could. One hit me here. *(Rubs her arm.)* They always do this. Can they get in the window?

MARTIN: Who? Who? What are they doing? Who are *they*?

JUDITH: It's those rough boys. They chase us and throw stones. I had to go across the river to take the tea for my mother. The lady wouldn't take the tea. She said I had insulted her. But I didn't. I only said what was true.

MARTIN: What was she angry about?
JUDITH: I'll tell you just how it was. Here she was behind her counter with the laces on it. And in I came with the tea. I put it down on the counter — it is such a high counter. I say, "Here is the tea you ordered." She picks up the package, smells it, takes the string off, and she spills it all over the counter. She picks up some more and puts it in her mouth; then she looks so red, and she says very angry and very loud, "This is not the tea I ordered. Your mother has cheated me. This is worse than any tea I ever tasted." But that was not true. It cannot be, for she buys the worst there is, so cheap, and so I tell her, just as it really is, "No, that is not true; it cannot be worse than the tea you ordered. There is no tea worse than what you always buy."

Why should she be so angry at that? But she was. She swept the tea all back in the paper and pushed it at me, and she screamed to me, loud and angry, to take it back, and she would never buy any more of my mother's tea as long as she should live. My mother will be so sorry. And she will cry, because the money was to pay the rent. (*The girl crumples down in a heap, crying.*)

MARTIN: Come, come! Things are not so bad as you think they are. Come over to the fire, and warm your hands. They are so cold. You would have things worse than they really are. Come. Come over here. (*Picks up package of tea.*) Does it cost so very much, this tea? I have none, and I shall have to buy some. I like good tea; it is a luxury I give myself. But I do not need good tea. Any tea can warm me and make me comfortable.

JUDITH (*looking up eagerly*): Do you want to buy it? It is not bad tea at all. It is really very good tea. And it is so cheap. Only two little coins for all of this.

MARTIN (*counting out coins*): Yes, yes, I think I shall need it. Thank you, and tell your mother I may need some more some time. If you are along this way, will you bring it to me?

JUDITH: Yes, yes. Good-bye. Thank you, thank you. Good-bye. (*Judith dashes out the door and away. Martin looks out the window.*)

MARTIN: Christmas Eve is nearly over. . .and I have not seen the Christ-child.

(*Discouraged, he picks up the stool and places it so the light from the candle shines on it.*)

But then, He could hardly see my small light when there are so many bright ones for Him.

(*He takes his Bible from the table, sits on the stool, opens the Bible, and reads. It is very quiet. From offstage comes a crescendo of music, "It Came Upon a Midnight Clear" played on a harp.*)

VOICE (*offstage*): Martin! (*Music grows faint.*) Martin!

MARTIN (*looking up from his Bible*): Who art thou? (*Then he listens intently.*)

	The Least of These
VOICE	I was hungered, and ye gave Me meat; I was thirsty, and ye gave Me drink; I was a stranger, and ye took Me in; naked, and ye clothed Me. Inasmuch as ye have done it unto the least of these, my brethern, ye have done it unto me.
	(*Martin listens as if spellbound. The music swells again, and the stage grows dark.*)

[THE END]

SUGGESTIONS FOR THE DIRECTOR

Regarding Rehearsal and Production of *The Least of These*

This play can fill your need for either an all-boy or all-girl cast as well as a mixed one. The needs, longings, and satisfactions of these characters are so universal that they may be adapted to players of either sex. When girls played all the roles they made these changes: Martin, the shoemaker, became Marta, the seamstress; Stephen, the street cleaner, was renamed Stella, the charwoman; and Peter was changed to Anna. The girls left the soldier and Nichol unchanged and found they could give convincing interpretations of these two male characters.

When boys do the play they change Catherine and Elsbeth to old Dmitri and his little grandson. As a substitute for Catherine's telling that her husband is away at war Dmitri mentions that his son, the little boy's father, is at the war. The boys change Lenore to Yosef, Peter's brother. The apple vendor becomes a man, an old man. Judith, the tea seller, is changed to Leon, the tea seller. Like Judith he is frightened by a gang of boys and takes refuge in Martin's shop. Such changes make the play ideal for presentation by either a boys' or girls' club.

In addition to its suitability for both sexes the play challenges the interest of many age groups, from ten-year-olds through teenagers, even to adults. No matter who the players are they have here a chance to act one of the classics of world literature. Leo Tolstoi, author of the play's story, used to say to his children, "Everything that matters is inside your minds and hearts." In this story he shows the truth of his words. Its plot does not grow out of physical conflict, but out of the changes that occur in the characters' minds and hearts.

The success of this play depends on how well players show the characters' changing thoughts and feelings. In the beginning of the play comes Martin. He thinks about his dream of the night before. His mood is one of awe as he wonder whether the Voice of his dream was real, and whether its words will come true. As director of the play you will need to help Martin convey this feeling. Offstage music at the play's opening can help him and create atmosphere to put the audience in the mood of the scene. Carolers might sing a solemn Christmas carol, the type of "It Came upon a Midnight Clear." Equally effective would be the same carol played on violin or piano. In addition to creating atmosphere this music is a device to get the immediate attention of the audience. Music continues during Martin's pantomime, grows fainter when he speaks, and ceases as Stephen enters.

Throughout the play Martin's dream flashes across his mind, even when he is absorbed by the problems of his visitors. He shows these thoughts by frequent glances out the window. Each glance should be planned both for timing and intensity. Of course he looks just before a visitor asks if he expects some one, or why he gazes at the window. He varies the intensity and the length of his glances. At times he merely turns his eyes or head in the direction of the window. Again, he turns his whole body toward it. He peers out and looks to the right and then to the left as he says, "Christmas Eve is almost over." Then he sighs as he gives up hope and says, "And I have not seen the Christ-child."

With the next line, "But then He could hardly see my small light," he looks at the candle and window for the last time. Then he turns away in humble resignation and puts on his glasses to enjoy his daily reading of the Bible.

Then comes the Voice, which is the play's climax and conclusion. If Martin shows ever-increasing interest in the window he increases the effect of the climax. He adds suspense by the changing emotions he shows in his speeches about his dream. At first he can hardly believe he had it. He shows this by the matter-of-fact way he answers Stephen. When Stephen asks, "Are you expecting someone?" Martin says simply, "Well, I hardly know." Then his hope begins to grow as he asks, "Do you really think I shall see Christ?" Hope expands even more when little Elsbeth suggests the candle in the window. He should show eagerness not only in his words but in his sudden smile and quickened step as he gets the candle.

Then his hope is dimmed by the Soldier, who makes fun of the candle. Martin shows this discouragement in his eyes and body as well as with the words, "Oh, that isn't nonsense."

On his speech, "Oh, sir, don't! Don't do that!" he moves with the greatest vigor and speaks with the greatest volume that he uses any time during the play. Make this movement to protect the candle a sharp contrast to Martin's usual gentle manner. At this moment the audience should catch its breath as it wonders what the Soldier will do to the candle.

In addition to building suspense toward the play's climax Martin helps build toward a minor climax in the scene with each of his visitors. He does this in part by sympathizing with the visitor's plight, trying to find a way to help, and finally by his relief and joy at improving the visitor's attitude and situation.

The visitors share equally in the responsibility to build

their scenes to a climax. First, by the way they enter the shop they should show something of what is in their hearts and minds. They also show how cold they are and how they welcome the warmth of Martin's shop. Each by his manner of entering gives a hint of his personality and problem. Here are examples: Stephen leaning on his snow stained shovel and hobbling in reveals that he is old and weary and has been doing hard physical labor. Catherine clutching under her chin the ends of the kerchief that covers her head and hesitating in the doorway shows her timidity and desperation. Elsbeth clinging to her mother's skirt for both warmth and moral support portrays her shyness and need of warm clothing.

The Soldier swaggering and looking down on humble Martin shows his insolence and disregard for everyone but himself. Marya displays her vigor and belief in firm discipline as she holds Nichol by the ear and drags him screaming and fighting to get free. Peter and Lenore with their half-skipping, half-running step as they bring in the yule log and bowl of wheat offer relief in the happiness of carefree childhood. The Kalend Singers offer similar relief with their quick movement and merry greetings in addition to their song. Judith crying for help dashes into the shop so the audience immediately sees her young strength and volatile temperament.

In the first rehearsals question your players to help them think about what their characters are like. Ask what they can do to portray these characteristics and the changes that Martin effects in each visitor. The climax of each scene is in the change of mood and attitude of the visitor, so make the changes obvious. Attention may be focused on a change in the visitor's heart or mind by some of the following: a long pause; a big gesture; a movement across the stage; new facial expression; change in tone of voice; change in tempo of speaking; and a change of posture. Most of the changes do not occur suddenly. Guide players in taking time to show what is happening in their minds. In each scene Martin's emotions also change, usually from worry to satisfaction or even joy in knowing he has been of help. He also must use eyes, face, hands, and body as well as words to portray the transitions of feeling and thought.

To make sure the audience sees the actors' pantomime be careful to arrange entrances and stage properties as described in the script. The entrance up left permits Martin to face the audience as he enters and crosses to the window. Spectators can see his expressions of wonder and doubt. The entrance midway on the right that leads outdoors gives visitors the chance to face the audience as they enter. Martin can encourage this by standing below them. This means he is nearer the audience than they are, so as they look at him the audience can see their faces. He can almost turn his back to the audience as visitors enter, for the audience has seen his face and now wants a look at the newcomer. The visitor naturally turns toward Martin, so if Martin is between the visitor and the audience the visitor's face will be plainly visible. A director once said to players who continually and without reason turned their backs to the audience, "Ordinarily your face is more expressive than the back of your head. So let the audience see your face as you enter, and let your face tell all it can about your character."

The fireplace and workbench on the opposite side of the room from the outside entrance give visitors a reason to walk across the stage. They want to warm themselves or sit on the bench. Walking there lets them show through their posture and manner of waking something more about their character than their speech tells. Inexperienced players tend to huddle near the entrance. They should not do this unless there is a dramatic reason for it. An example of the latter is Catherine, who hesitates near the entrance because of her shyness and poverty.

The offstage Voice since it provides the high moment of the play should be carefully rehearsed. It should not be recognizable as the voice of any actor or of the director. To impart a superhuman quality the Voice may use a megaphone or microphone. This does not mean it should be inordinately loud. Its words are spoken slowly, clearly, and with great tenderness.

The Voice should seem to come from offstage up left. Martin turns toward the sound at its start, then sits motionless and spellbound until its conclusion. Music and light can add to the effectiveness of this climax. If you have a spotlight, focus it up center just before the Voice speaks. Turn off other stage lights. As the Voice concludes, the same music that opened the play should be heard again. It swells to a crescendo as Martin seeming to follow the Voice slowly rises and goes off left. After his exit the music dies out.

Impress upon all offstage players the need for absolute quiet during the entire play, but most importantly during this final scene. Any offstage sound other than the music can completely destroy the play's illusion. Insist upon this silence at rehearsals as well as during performance.

You may elaborate your production of this play with song and dance. The script suggests a song by the Kalend Singers. If they dance while singing they will give life and contrast to the performance. Another interlude of singing and dancing may be included if Peter and Lenore are accompanied by a group of boys and girls. All of them dance to the accompaniment of their own song just before they leave. Such numbers not only enliven the performance, but they also give opportunity for additional young people to participate.

The stage set for this play is easily arranged. Almost any neutral background will serve if you add a window and fireplace. Players have often presented this little drama in one end of a room that had a convenient fireplace on one side and a window on the other. If such space is not available build a fireplace of apple boxes securely fastened together. Cover their surface with papier-mâché stones, and paint the surface to look as if mortar had fallen away in several places. Be sure to provide a firmly anchored hook on which to hang the tea kettle. Create a glow in the fireplace by placing there a flashlight partially covered with coarsely fringed sections of red, yellow, and orange, flame-proofed crepe paper.

The picture over the mantle can be a Madonna or head of Christ. It has a very simple frame or none at all.

The window is even more essential than the fireplace. It should not be large, and may be high to suggest that Martin's shop is in a basement. If you can't do better, paint a window on the center panel of a screen.

The workbench, table, small bench, and stool should appear old and poor and worn. Don't use a modern chrome and leather kitchen ladder stool. Better than this would be an old wooden chair without its back. You can give some color to an otherwise drab scene if you place brightly colored mugs and teapot on the open shelves up center. These should suggest a long-ago peasant home of eastern Europe. The tea in the cannister on the cupboard shelf is loose, not in modern, individual, ready to use tea bags. The bread that Martin offers Catherine should not be a modern, presliced, plastic wrapped loaf. It should be more like today's long or round loaf of Vienna or French bread.

Real water is in the kettle at the fireplace. Martin uses it when he makes tea. He and his visitors practice with both tea leaves and water at several rehearsals. They know at precisely what moment to pour or drink. They time this business so it will add and not detract from the effectiveness of their speeches. A poorly timed drink during performance can cause a player to choke or giggle. Prevent this by exact timing of the business and repeated rehearsal of it.

Make the most of all hand properties, and be sure they are in the right place and ready for use. Marya has her basket of apples; Stephen, his shovel; Judith, the paper bag of tea; Peter, a small yule log; Lenore, a bowl of wheat; Kalend Singers, their wands decorated with colored paper streamers; and the Soldier, his sword hanging from his belt.

Ready onstage for Martin's use are the tea cannister, teapot, mugs, Christmas greens, bread, and a knife for slicing it. The tea kettle of water hangs over the fireplace. On the table are his glasses, the shoe he mends, an awl, and small hammer or coarse thread and large needle, and his Bible. The coat or jacket he gives to Catherine is on the stool or bench. On the shelf are coins in a little dark bag and the candle for Elsbeth. This should be a flashlight candle. Martin practices lighting it by holding it near the fire. Then he shields the light as though shielding a flame as he carries it to Elsbeth.

All hand properties should be available from the fourth rehearsal on. This early practice gives players ideas for characterization and develops their skill and confidence in using properties.

You will note in *The Least of These* some of the same advantages and challenges as in *The Toymaker's Doll:* The main character is so important to the play that you should rehearse two players in the role and give each a chance to perform for an audience. Since other players appear for only short scenes you can schedule their rehearsals so they do not have long waits. Refer to Suggestions for the Director following *The Toymaker's Doll* for detailed procedures.

The basic costumes are similar for characters in the two plays. On the whole, costumes for *The Least of These* are poorer and less colorful. Catherine and Elsbeth wear no wraps except kerchiefs on their heads. Stephen has strips of cloth around his legs to hold his trousers close as protection against the cold. He wears a shawl over his head and shoulders and fastened at the throat. Wearing similar shawsl are Marya, Judith, and Lenore. Peter and Nichol wear round caps. Kalend Singers wear an assortment of shawls, capes, and hoods. Martin wears the smock and long trousers of a peasant man. They are nondescript in color. A little grey in his hair and a few lines in his face indicate he is no longer young.

You can find suggestions for starting rehearsals by letting players act the play's story in *Creative Children's Theatre for Home, School, Church, and Playground.** In the book's chapter on story play are procedures for acting the story, "Where Love Is, God Is." This is the story that is dramatized in *The Least of These.*

---

*Maxine McSweeny, *Creative Children's Theatre for Home, School, Church, and Playground* (South Brunswick and New York: A. S. Barnes and Co., 1974).

Santa! Please Get Up!

by Maxine McSweeny

CHARACTERS:

DUMPLING, Santa's cook
CREAM PUFF, her young helper
SANTA CLAUS
MISS GOODE, Santa's secretary
MRS. CORLETT, a doting mother
SUZETTE, her daughter
LYNNE, a little girl
CYNTHIA
CAROL — artists, who work for Santa
MILLY
DICK, the reindeer groom
DOCTOR HEALEM
BEN
ROY — paramedics

TIME: *Christmas Eve.*

SCENE: *Santa's home. Up right an entrance leads outdoors. Down right is a worktable with two stools behind it. On the table are stacks of small paper bags, a jar of cookies, and Santa's bag of lunch. A cot is along the left side of the stage, its head about center, and its foot down left. There is room for a player to walk along the left side of the cot.*

At its head is a pillow. A red cover is neatly folded on the foot of the cot. From off right comes the sound of wooden spoons beating against mixing bowls. The spoons sound the rhythm of the Mother Goose Rhyme, "A Pat-a-Cake, a-Pat-a-Cake, a Baker's Man."

Dumpling and Cream Puff enter, each beating a spoon against a bowl. As they beat they speak the rhyme with great enthusiasm. Continuing to speak and beat they go down right and stand behind the table.

DUMPLING
CREAM PUFF A-pat-cake, a-pat-acake, a Christmas cake,
       Cookies, and tarts we put in to bake.
       Roll them, and stir them for children to eat
       And put them in the stockings for a Santa Claus treat.

(*After speaking the rhyme once they put bowls & spoons on the table and turn to face each other. They repeat the rhyme and clap hands as if playing a game of Bean Porridge Hot.*)

(*While they are playing, Santa enters. Yawning and stretching he goes to the cot and sits on the edge of it. He shakes his head as if trying to shake off drowsiness, then looks admiringly at the cooks. They are so busy with their game they do not notice him until he speaks.*)

SANTA: Are the cookies ready?

CREAM PUFF: Not quite. (*running to him*) But don't worry. They will be ready.

DUMPLING: You want enough for every stocking, don't you?

SANTA (*pulling off his boots and putting them behind the head of the cot*): I don't know (*yawns*) whether I do or not. I'm so tired I can't think.

CREAM PUFF: Well we can. And we'll have them ready, won't we, Dumpling?

DUMPLING: Yes, we will, Cream Puff. We surely will.
SANTA: I'll just close my eyes a minute while you finish. (*He lies down on the cot.*)
DUMPLING (*stirring vigorously and starting to speak the rhyme again*): A-pat-acake, a-pat-acake, a Christmas cake,

CREAM PUFF
and   Cookies, and tarts we put in to bake.
DUMPLING   Roll them and stir them for the children to eat,
                       And put them in the stockings for a Santa Claus treat.

CREAM PUFF (*noticing Santa on the cot*): What's he doing that for?
DUMPLING: I guess he wants a rest.
CREAM PUFF: Rest! So do I. So does everybody. But we can't. Not on Christmas Eve.
DUMPLING (*taking cookies from the jar and putting them in the paper bags*): Well, he knows that better than anybody. He certainly does.
(*A loud knock is heard off right. Mrs. Corlett peeks in, draws back, and steps inside.*)
MRS. C.: I know we shouldn't do this. (*She walks boldly to center. Suzette follows holding a doll carelessly by one of its arms.*) But may we come in?
CREAM PUFF (*looking first at Mrs. C. and then at Dumpling*): What are they doing here?
DUMPLING: I don't know. I certainly don't know.
CREAM PUFF (*going toward Mrs. C.*) Aren't you in the wrong place?
MRS. C.: Well, it's none of my business, but isn't this Santa's house?
DUMPLING: Yes, it is. It certainly is.

CREAM PUFF: But he can't have visitors tonight. He has to leave.
MRS. C. (*with a sight of relief*): O thank goodness! He hasn't gone yet. I was afraid we'd miss him.
SUZETTE (*crossing in front of Cream Puff to table*): Whose cookies are those?
DUMPLING: The children's. All the children Santa will visit tonight.
SUZETTE (*boldly*): If you'd ask me, I'd take one.
CREAM PUFF: We can't. They're not our cookies.
SUZETTE (*grabbing a cookie and running up center*): Then I'll take one anyway.
MRS. C.: Oh, Suzette! (*She follows Suzette and puts a loving hand on the child's shoulder.*) You just love cookies, don't you, dear? (*Suzette's mouth is too full to answer, but she nods vigorously. Cream Puff looks disapprovingly at Suzette, then goes to the table and puts the lid on the cookie jar.*)
DUMPLING: Here! (*Cream Puff pushes the jar toward Dumpling, who puts it in her lap for safekeeping.*) I'll take care of it.
MRS. C.: (*leading Suzette toward table*): We came because we want to talk to Santa. (*As Dumpling sees Suzette approach Dumpling puts both arms around the cookie jar and holds it close to her.*)
CREAM PUFF (*to Mrs. C.*) You can't talk to him now. He has to leave to deliver the children's presents. He wants to surprise them.
SUZETTE: I don't want another surprise. (*She dangles the doll in front of her*) Look what he brought me last year—a baby doll. I'm no baby.

MRS. C. (*to Cream Puff and Dumpling*): You see, Suzette is so smart for her age! Aren't you honey?
SUZETTE: Yes, I am. Mama, tell them that cute thing I said on the way here.
MRS. C.: Oh, yes! She said, "Mama, a baby doll's for babies. I'm getting grown-up, so I want a grown-up doll." Wasn't that the cutest thing? (*Mrs. C. and Suzette laugh loudly enough to wake Santa. He turns over and looks at them.*)
SANTA: What's going on here? Who are these visitors?
MRS. C. (*taking a step or two toward the cot*): Oh, Santa! I'm Mrs. Corlette. (*She takes Suzette's hands and leads her to the cot.*) And this is my darling, little Suzette.
SUZETTE: Are you the real Santa Claus?
SANTA (*sitting up*): I'm real to me. (*Holds out his arm*) Pinch me, and see if I'm real to you.
SUZETTE (*giving his arm a big pinch*): I will.
SANTA (*drawing back with the pain of her pinch*): Ow! Wow! What a pinch!
SUZETTE (*pleased with herself*): I'm strong. Mama, tell him how strong I am.
SANTA (*rubbing his arm*) Never mind. I believe you.
MRS. C.: Now, Santa, maybe it's none of my business, but we've come to talk about Suzette's Christmas present.
SUZETTE (*holding out doll*): I don't want another doll like this. I want one with some hair.
MRS. C.: You see, Santa, children today are smarter than they used to be. They want more grown-up presents, and well—well—something better.

SUZETTE (*whirling the doll around by its one arm*): Yes. Something better than this old thing.
MRS. C.: You understand, don't you santa?
SANTA (*horrified as he looks at Suzette's treatment of the doll*): I'm afraid I do. You don't need to tell me any more.
MRS. C.: Oh, thank you, Santa. I thought you'd understand. Now, it's none of my business, but shouldn't you get started?
SANTA (*his thoughts far away*): I suppose I should.
MRS. C. (*taking Suzette's hand and starting toward entrance*): Come, Suzette, we must go home before Santa gets there.
SUZETTE (*pulling Mrs. C. toward table*): I want another cookie. (*Dumpling holds the jar close to her. Cream Puff steps in front of her to protect the jar. Suzette seeing she cannot get a cookie follows her mother up right.*)
MRS. C. (*at entrance*): Goodbye.
SUZETTE,(*still holding Mrs. C's hand draws back and sticks out her tongue*): I don't like your cookies anyway. (*They go.*)
SANTA: So they want something better—and something more grown-up. They don't like my presents. That settles it. I'm too tired to go tonight. Nobody cares, so I'll just sleep. And I won't wake up til Christmas is over. (*He lies down, pulls the red cover over his head, and turns toward the wall.*)
CREAM PUFF (*to Dumpling*): Did you see that?
DUMPLING: I did. I certainly did.
CREAM PUFF: What are you going to do?
DUMPLING: Not a thing. Not a little teeny thing.
CREAM PUFF: We have to do something. He can't lie there on Christmas Eve.

DUMPLING (*packing cookies*):	Our job is to pack cookies. And we better get it done.
CREAM PUFF:	What's the use if he doesn't deliver them?
DUMPLING:	Don't worry. He will. He certainly will. (*Enter Miss Goode. She carries a very short pencil and a clipboard with many papers attached. She shuffles through them often and makes notes about what is said and done. She stops up center and looks at her wristwatch, then looks at the cooks.*)
MISS G.:	Dumpling! How many cookies have you packed?
CREAM PUFF:	Well, let's see. We have— we have— we must have— (*to Dumpling*) How many do we have Dumpling?
DUMPLING:	About a million.
MISS G. (*making a note*):	About a million. (*She breaks her pencil lead*) Look at that! I never break a pencil. I've used this one all year. (*As she talks she peels back little splinters of wood to expose the end of the lead.*) Some people are always sharpening pencils. That just wastes them. I can't stand waste. I say, "Use it up, wear it out. Make it do, or do without." (*Triumphantly holds up pencil to show tiny point of lead.*) Now! Look! Good as new. And I didn't need a pencil sharpener either.
DUMPLING:	That's a blessing. Not enough pencil there to get in a sharpener.
MISS G. (*paying no attention to Dumpling as she looks at her papers*):	Santa's lunch! Is it packed?
DUMPLING:	It is. (*Points to bag on the table*) It certainly is.
MISS G.:	And when will the last cookies be packed.

DUMPLING: On time. They'll be packed on time.
CREAM PUFF: But what does "on time" mean? Santa's not going.
MISS G.: Oh yes he is. (*Looks at her clipboard then at her watch.*) And in just five minutes. (*Checking items on clipboard papers as she speaks.*) I've checked with the artists. Every toy is painted and loaded. I've checked with Dick. The reindeer are harnessed. And I think Santa's in the driveway right now.
DUMPLING: That's what you think. But that's not where he is.
MISS G.: I better check him. (*Starts toward entrance.*)
CREAM PUFF (*darting in front of Miss Goode to block her exit*): Wait! Miss Goode! He's here. (*Crosses to cot.*) Under these covers. Look!
MISS G.: Who's that?
CREAM PUFF: It's Santa.
MISS G.: It can't be.
CREAM PUFF: Well, it is.
MISS G. (*going to cot and calling*): Santa! (*louder*) Santa! Are you asleep?
SANTA (*pulling covers away from his face so he can speak, but not looking around*): Yes. I'm asleep. I'm sound asleep.
MISS G.: You can't be. It's time for you to go.
SANTA: I'm not going. I'm tired, and I'm going to sleep.
MISS G.: What about the toys?
SANTA: Nobody wants my toys.
DUMPLING: Yes, they do, and you don't want to disappoint the children.

SANTA (*sitting up and looking at Dumpling*): They won't be disappointed. You heard that little Suzette. They want something better—something grown-up. Well let them go to the store and buy their presents. I'm not delivering any. I'm staying home and sleeping. You understand? I'm not going. (*Pulls cover and lies down.*)

MISS G.: Not at all?

DUMPLING: You don't mean it.

CREAM PUFF: What will we do?

(*The three move slowly to the work table as they whisper together. From off right comes the sound of singing. Milly, Carol, and Cynthia, each carrying a long slender paint brush, skip in. To the tune of "Jingle Bells" they are singing the following words:*)

ARTISTS: Jingle bells, jingle bells, jingle all the way. Oh, what fun it is to paint the toys for Santa's sleigh.
We've painted every one;
And now our work is done;
And so we've come to celebrate
No matter if it's late. Hi!

(*As they shout the final "Hi!" they wave their paint brushes and skip to different parts of the room. Cynthia goes to the foot of Santa's cot, Carol to its head, and Milly, up center.*)

CYNTHIA: We're late, but we've painted the last doll face.

CAROL: And the last picture book.

MILLY: And they're all on the sleigh.

CYNTHIA: Where's Santa?
MISS G.: Look beside you.
(*The three artists look at the cot.*)
MISS G.: That's Santa.
CREAM PUFF: He won't get up.
CAROL: He better. It's late. Is he asleep?
MISS G.: He says he is.
MILLY: Then he's fooling. (*Runs to foot of cot.*) I know how to get him up. Here, Cynthia. We'll tickle his feet.
(*They lift the edge of the cover and tickle Santa's feet.*)
MILLY:
Tickle, tickle, tickle! Tickle, tickle, tickle!
CYNTHIA:
SANTA (*kicking wildly*): Stop! You're tickling! Stop!
(*Milly and Cynthia quickly step back where he cannot reach them. Cynthia runs up center rubbing her arm where she felt Santa's kick. Santa tucks the cover under his feet, lies down, and again pulls the cover over his head. Milly and Cynthia join Carol up center where the three huddle together for protection.*)
CAROL: What a kick!
CYNTHIA: I didn't know he was so strong.
MISS G. (*making a note*): Tickling didn't work.
MILLY: He can't get away with this. Let's pull off his cover. Come on Cynthia.
CYNTHIA: I'm afraid. Carol, you go.
MILLY: There's nothing to be afraid of. Stay on this side. I'll go over there. (*She goes to the far side of the cot. Carol reluctantly follows Milly's instructions.*) Sneak up

Santa! Please Get Up! 109

slowly. Sh! Sh! (*Each grabs a top corner of the cover. They pull, but Santa is too quick for them. He pulls the cover out of their hands.*)

SANTA: Oh, no, you don't. Now I just want a little sleep, and I mean to have it. You better leave me alone. (*Disappointed, Carol and Milly tiptoe up left to join Cynthia.*)

MISS G. (*making a note*): Stealing covers didn't work.

(*From off right comes the sound of sleigh bells. Dick enters. He carries reins to which are attached a few sleigh bells that jingle merrily as he walks.*)

DICK (*entering and yelling like a college cheer leader*): A-a-aal-ll ready! A-a-aal-ll ready!

MISS G.: Well, we're not already.

DICK: Oh yes, we are. I've hitched the reindeer. They're just waiting for me to put the jingles on. (*Shakes bells.*) Where's Santa?

DUMPLING: That's a good question. A very good question.

CREAM PUFF (*frantic*): He's asleep. Look over there.

DICK: I must get him up. It's time to go.

MISS G. (*looking at her watch*): It's time to go all right. And I'd like to see you get him up.

DICK (*going to cot and shaking bells near Santa's ear*): Santa! SANTA! (*Santa does not move.*) What's the matter?

MISS GOODE: Maybe he can't hear you.

DICK (*bending close to Santa*): S-A-N-T-A! (*Turns to others*) I can't yell any louder.

CREAM PUFF: I know how to make it louder. (*She picks up a paper bag from the table, rolls it into a cone shape so it resembles a megaphone, and hands it to Dick. He puts the big end near Santa's ear and yells into the other end.)*

DICK: SANTA! PLEASE GET UP! (*to others*) I can't make him hear. Please help me. (*Quickly Cream Puff passes paper bags to the others. They roll their own paper megaphones, crowd around Santa and yell.*)

ALL: SANTA! PLEASE GET UP!

DICK: He's gone deaf. I'll get Dr. Healem. (*All move back to the places they had before yelling.*)

MISS GOODE (*writing*): Yelling. Didn't work.

CREAM PUFF: Why do you keep writing what doesn't work?

MISS GOODE: So we won't make the same mistake again. If you don't learn by experience, you never learn.

CREAM PUFF: Dumpling, what can we do? You don't seem worried.

DUMPLING: I'm not. He'll go when he's ready. He certainly will!

MISS G.: I say we should forget the whole thing. Let him sleep. It's wasteful to have Christmas every year. Once every two years would be enough for me. If he doesn't go, we'll have all the toys ready for next year.

CAROL: You mean we'll have a year's vacation?

MISS G.: Well, something like that.

CYNTHIA: I'm tired enough to take a year off.

CREAM PUFF: I don't like it. I want Christmas every year.

MILLY: Here comes Dr. Healem.
(*Enter Dr. Healem carrying a little black bag. Dick follows.*)
DR. H. (*to everybody*): Good evening.
ALL: Good evening. How do you do, Dr. Healem. Thank you for coming.
DR. H. (*looking around*): Where's the patient?
DICK (*dashing to head of cot*): Right here, Doctor.
CREAM PUFF (*pushing stool from behind table*): Will you need this?
DICK (*carrying stool to cot*): Oh yes. Here, Dr. Healem. Won't you sit on this?
DR. H. (*sitting*): Thank you. (*All watch silently and attentively as Dr. H. opens his little black bag. He takes out a stethoscope and listens to Santa's chest and then his ear. Dr. looks carefully at the ear.*) His ear's all right. He must have sleeping sickness. We have to get him awake. Call the paramedics.
DICK: The paramedics! (*He darts toward entrance*) I'll get them. (*He hurries out.*)
MISS G. (*writing*): Doctor couldn't wake him.
CREAM PUFF (*approaching Dr. H. as he puts his stethoscope in the bag*): Dr. Healem.
DR. H.: What is it, child?
CREAM PUFF: Is Santa sick?
(*Everyone listens eagerly for his answer.*)
DR. H.: I can't tell until I get some tests. But we have to wake him. I think the paramedics can do it.
(*Siren sounds off right.*)
ALL: Here they come. It didn't take long. Good old paramedics. I hope they can wake him.
(*Enter Roy and Ben carrying their equip-

ment and ready for action. They move fast but hesitate up center.)
ROY: Did you call the paramedics?
ALL: Yes. Over there. On the cot.
BEN: Is that the patient?
DR. H.: Right here, gentlemen.
(*Dr. H. steps left of the foot of the cot so the audience has a good view of Roy and Ben as they work at the side of the cot.*)
DICK (*entering and hurrying up left and standing just above the cot*):
I see you got here all right.
(*Roy nods. Ben puts oxygen mask over Santa's face. The mask is connected by a tube or cord to a tire pump that Roy puts on the floor beside the cot. Roy pumps as though pumping air into a tire.*)
LYNNE (*calling off right*): Santa Claus! (*Almost sobbing*) Oh! Oh! Santa Claus!
MILLY (*looking off right*): There's a child out here.
DUMPLING: If it's that little Suzette, don't let her in.
CREAM PUFF (*going to entrance*): She's the cause of all the trouble.
(*Lynne enters hesitantly and stands just inside.*)
CREAM PUFF: What's the matter, child?
(*All, even Ben and Roy, stop to listen for Lynne's answer.*)
LYNNE: I want Santa. I have to find him.
CREAM PUFF: Why do you want Santa?
LYNNE: For my little brother and sister. You see we live close by. Santa always stops at our house first. He didn't come tonight. My

Santa! Please Get Up!

brother and sister are crying. They want Santa.

(*Santa pushes off the oxygen mask and swings around to sit on the side of the cot. Ben and Roy get their pump out of the way and stand near Dick.*)

SANTA: What's that? Does somebody want me?

LYNNE (*sobbing*): Oh! Oh! Santa! Please come.

SANTA: Don't cry. Come here, child. What's the matter?

LYNNE (*trying to hold back her tears as she goes to Santa*): Oh! Oh! (*Santa takes her hand and shows she is to sit beside him. She sits between him and the audience so when he looks at her he does not see what the others are doing.*)

SANTA: Tell me all about it. Don't cry. I can't stand crying.

(*Miss G. hears this, gets an idea, and quietly moves up center. There she beckons all the others to join her. She begins to cry and signals to the others to do the same. Even Roy and Ben, and finally Dr. Healem join the group and add their "boo-hoo's" to the others. The crying is so loud that no one can hear what Lynne says to Santa. He listens and comforts her. Then he becomes aware of all the crying and turns to look at the others.*)

SANTA: Don't cry. Please! Don't cry. I'm going. Cream Puff, will you bring my boots?

LYNNE: Here! Let me help too.

(*Cream Puff gets the boots from above the cot. She and Lynn quickly help Santa get them on.*)

MISS G. (*writing*): Crying worked.
SANTA (*pulling on boots*) See! I'm going. I just wanted to know someone cared. (*He jumps up*) I'm up and ready. Dick, get the jingles on the reindeer.
(*Dick runs out. Santa takes Lynne's hand and leads her to the entrance. There he stops to give final orders.*)
SANTA: Dumpling, get the cookies on the sleigh. Miss Goode, check to see that everything's in order, and WE'RE OFF!
(*Lynne and Santa go.*)
DUMPLING: Here! Everyone of you! Carry out a bag of cookies.
(*Each one scurries to get a bag and hurry off right. As they start for the bags Dumpling says the first line of her Pat-a-Cake rhyme. All the others join in and speak the last lines with her. They repeat it until all but Miss Goode have gone off right. As they go Miss Goode frantically checks off pages on her clipboard. When she is the only one left onstage she notices Santa's lunch on the table.*)
MISS G: The lunch! Santa! Wait! Santa! Your lunch!
(*Still calling she picks it up and darts off right. A chorus of goodbye's is heard after she leaves the stage.*)
ALL (*off right*): Good-bye. Good-bye. Hurrah for Santa!
(*The sound quickly dies away.*)

[THE END]

SUGGESTIONS FOR THE DIRECTOR

Regarding Rehearsal and Production of *Santa! Please Get Up!*

Here is a play for young children, even six- and seven-year-olds, although it has appeal for children as old as ten. The play is a good choice for presentation at a children's party in a living room or on the lawn. It is also appropriate for several performances given for different classes in school or Sunday school. Children of this age should play before only small audiences and should be encouraged to give more than one performance. Very young players need to be close to the audience so they do not strain their voices or act in exaggerated ways unnatural to children.

Even children who are too young to present a play for an audience can have fun with this play. You can stimulate them to play at some of the activities depicted in the play. They can engage in this spontaneous play-acting without any director, rehearsal, or audience.

To get such play-acting started you first read the play to a group of children or tell them its story. Then all you need to do is make available some of the play's properties. Try to get some or all of the following: bowls and spoons; a doll; a pencil, clipboard, and sheets of paper; water color brushes, a strip of cloth with bells attached; toy kit with doctor's instruments; tire pump and hose or cord; cookies and small paper bags; and a piece of firm, hard plastic for oxygen mask.

Hearing the story and having the play properties will probably induce the players to play baker, secretary, mother and spoiled child, paramedic, or Santa Claus. If the children can use a sofa, bench, or chaise lounge they may want to play waking up Santa Claus and roll paper megaphones through which to call him. Boys and girls often continue such play for hours without help or guidance from adults.

Making or decorating items for this play gives incentive for craft activities suited to the interests and abilities of young children. They can decorate paper bags with paint or crayons. They may want to help bake cookies, mold them of clay, or cut out paper disks and color them to simulate cookies. Other crafts suggested by the play are sewing bells on strips of cloth, contriving an oxygen mask out of stiff plastic (not the thin plastic in dry cleaners' bags because of danger of suffocation), and making a stethoscope with black cord and ear plugs.

You may provide opportunity for crafts and a session of this same type of play-acting even for children who will later rehearse the play and present it for an audience. These players can make properties before or after rehearsal or while waiting their turns to rehearse. Their own impromptu play-acting can occur immediately after you first read the play to them and before they begin to rehearse.

Spontaneous play-acting suggested by the play helps young players think about the play and the feelings of its characters. Their initial contact with the play is one of free and undirected enjoyment. This helps sustain their interest through the period of rehearsals. It also makes for sincere and enthusiastic acting, which contributes to players' learning and often results in a more natural and spirited performance.

Once you start rehearsals you want players to realize they no longer act whatever they want to act, which they did in their impromptu play-acting. Rehearsals offer a different kind of pleasure. It is the thrill of working as a team toward the goal of giving a good performance. With the beginning of rehearsals, players accept the guidance of the director and the discipline of working as a team.

Santa! Please Get Up! demands extraordinary teamwork. Several players are onstage during most of the play. Each one practices until he can contribute to the performance every minute he is onstage. This is true whether he is speaking or not.

As director, you explain that players are never there merely to watch or listen to others. Each is there for just one purpose. That is to help tell the story of the play. If only one player neglects this he prevents the play from being as good as it should be.

Your players can achieve this kind of supportive acting only if you give direction for it and rehearse them in it. Devote some attention at each rehearsal to helping players act when they have no lines to speak.

As a beginning aid to acting at such times tell players to look at the player who is speaking. Explain the need for this. The audience tends to look where the players look. Give an example. Say to the players, "When you see a person looking intently at some object or at some other person, don't you turn at once to see what he is looking at? And don't you look even more eagerly if you see several people with their gaze fixed on the same object? Try standing on the corner and looking steadily down the street. You can expect every passerby to look in the direction you are looking."

Spectators at a play have this same impulse. They watch what the players watch. If one negligent actor looks away from the most important thing happening on the stage he distracts at least some members of the audience.

Looking at the speaker or at the actor whose pantomime is telling the story at the moment is the first step in acting when not speaking. The second step is to help players show how they feel about what is being said or done. This is an important part of an actor's pantomime. To develop this ability help players decide exactly what their characters would be thinking when not speaking. You may suggest actual words that might be going through a character's mind as he listens to another player. Ask a player, "What is your character saying to himself?" If the player has no answer, ask more questions: "Is your character thinking, 'Now Santa will surely go.' or is he wondering, 'What can we do to get him to go?' " After the player answers, tell him, "Now act as if you were thinking that."

Read through the script, and make note of what characters are thinking when not speaking. Discuss these notes with the players. Help them to show through their pantomime the thoughts and feelings of all characters throughout the play. The pantomime may be no more than an expression in the eyes or a turn of the head. It should never distract attention from the speaker, but rather help focus attention on him.

With your help your players are learning two important principles of supportive acting: (1) They look at the speaker or whatever is the most important thing happening on the stage at the moment. (2) They show their thoughts or feelings about what is being said or done. But all characters do not react in the same way or at exactly the same time.

So each palyer considers how his character reacts during the ever-changing situations of a play. Then his pantomime portrays these reactions. This pantomime is one way he shows what kind of person his character is, and so he helps bring the play to life. To help the actors give convincing interpretations of the characters in this play, here are examples of its characters' thoughts and feelings.

DUMPLING frequently says to herself, "Santa will go. Don't worry." She is older than the others. She does not move about as much as they do. Her experience makes her think, "Everything will be all right." She has other thoughts: "I'll get my job done." and "I like to say my Pat-a-Cake rhyme." You may be sure that she will have enough sacks ready for each player to carry one at play's end. She watches even more closely than others what is said and done, but she rarely moves from her stool.

CREAM PUFF is a contrast to Dumpling. She is young, excitable. Her thoughts are apt to be, "Oh, I'm so worried." "What shall we do if Santa won't go?" "The poor children—they will be so disappointed." "Will the doctor be able to wake Santa?" "How sick is he?" "Poor little Lynne!" She shows she loves everyone and loves the joy of Christmas.

MISS GOODE is determined above all else to do her job. Even in the midst of crisis she never forgets her clipboard and notes. From the moment she enters she is observing, planning, and writing. Her characteristic thoughts are: "Have I forgotten anything?" "Oh, I must see about something else." "Now what else can we do to get Santa awake?" At the climax she thinks, "Santa can't stand crying. I've an idea. I'll get the others to help. We'll all cry. That will get him started." This is one time when players do not look at the speaker. What Santa and Lynne are talking about is not as important as what Miss Goode is thinking. To get the audience to look at her she makes a quick move to center stage. Other players except Santa and Lynne look at Miss Goode. They watch her as she gets her idea. She looks straight at the audience to show she has a plan. Then she makes another big movement as she hurries up center. Other players are watching her and so are ready to respond to her signal to gather around her. She makes excited gestures as she shows in pantomime that she wants everyone to cry.

MILLY, CYNTHIA, and CAROL are young and eager for Christmas, but they are tired from their hard work. They react as a group. Staying close together they frequently look at one another as if to say, "What do you think of that?" or 'I think so too." During much of the play they stand up left and watch what others do. Milly is their leader. Carol and Cynthia look to her for a clue as to how they should feel about what happens. Before Milly tickles Santa's feet or pulls off his cover she thinks, "I've an idea." "Let's have some fun." "Let's try this."

DICK shows at all times what a reliable helper he is. When anything is to be done his first thought is, "I'll do it." He should show he thinks this *before* he says or does it. His self-confidence shows in the way he approaches a task. He frequently thinks, "I know what to do." or "I can do whatever needs to be done."

DOCTOR HEALEM shows the tender concern of a good doctor for his patient. His thoughts are, "What is the matter with Santa?" "I'll examine him and discover the cause of his trouble." As he listens to the stethoscope and looks at Santa's ear he thinks, "I want to see and hear everything that will help." Then he thinks, "His chest sounds all right. His ear looks all right." His next thought is, "We must get Santa awake. We need the paramedics." When Cream Puff asks about Santa, Dr. Healem thinks, "I don't want to worry her." When Santa suddenly wakens, the doctor rejoices, "Oh he's better. He's awake." Dr. Healem is among the last to join the crying, but he could be thinking, "My patient is well. Now we'll have some fun."

BEN and ROY enter thinking, "We know just what to do in an emergency. Lead us to it." As they work they think, "We've done this many times, and we do it right." We don't waste any time." When Miss Goode beckons them to join the crying, they think, "What's going on here? What does she want us to do?" They soon understand and think, "We've finished our work. The patient is awake. Let's join the fun. We'll cry as hard as any others."

MRS. CORLETT, SUZETTE, and LYNNE are onstage such short times that they have to help sustain interest for only a few minutes. But in these minutes they must show thoughts and feelings when others are speaking. As Mrs. Corlett enters, her thoughts are something like, "I'll just do anything to see that Suzette gets what she wants for Christmas." Later she thinks, "Isn't Suzette cute to steal a cookie?" and "Santa's a little old-fashioned. I'll have to explain to him how things are today." And finally, "I have important things to do at home."

SUZETTE's thoughts are obvious, and almost every child has observed girls like her. She thinks only of herself, what she wants, and how she can get it. It will be easy to draw from the player good ideas of what Suzette is thinking.

LYNNE enters thinking, "What can I do? I must find Santa!" and again, "I must not cry, but what can I do?" When Santa speaks, she thinks, "There he is! Dear Santa!" It is important for her to show she thinks this *before* she says, "Oh, Santa! Please come!" Then her thoughts are "I'm so relieved. I must not cry." and later, "He will come. My troubles are over." She pays no attention to the crying of others. She just wants to tell Santa how pleased her brother and sister will be to see him. She expresses her thoughts to him even though no one but Santa can hear what she says.

SANTA, like the others, must show his thoughts and feelings when others speak. He is onstage almost every minute of the play, yet he does not speak often. On entering he shows he is tired before he says so. He is already thinking, "I'm so tired I don't know whether I can go tonight." "I can hardly keep awake." When Mrs. Corlett and Suzette let him know they don't like his toys he thinks, "All of my hard work is no use. I might as well sleep. I'm so disappointed I'll sleep right through Christmas Eve." When Milly tickles his feet he thinks, "Nobody will get me out tonight. Nobody cares, and I'll sleep." Then he hears Lynne. He thinks, "Did she say somebody wanted me?" "What a nice little girl!" "She cares. So do her brother and sister." "Well if children care, I'll go. I'm glad they care. I want to go."

Every player onstage except Santa and Lynn participates fully in the crying scene. It should start gradually with Miss Goode giving the first "Boo-hoo." Milly and Cream Puff are the first to join her. Then come Cynthia and Carol, followed immediately by Dumpling and Dick. Ben, Roy, and Dr. Healem come last. Even though all do not come at the same instant they gather quickly. As soon as all are there and in a compact group (not a line) Miss Goode steps to the right of the others and directs their crying like a conductor leading an orchestra. She watches Santa. As soon as he says, "I'm going," she gives the signal to stop crying. Only two or three boo-hoo's are heard after that. Probably these are sounded by Milly and Cream Puff.

The chorus of offstage "good-byes" should be loud and merry at first and quickly die away.

Costumes for this play present few problems. Santa wears the traditional red suit. He wears a beard, but no mask. Dumpling and Cream Puff can wear their own dresses plus chef caps and aprons. Miss Goode should wear a dress of her mother's or other adult's. Carol and Cynthia and Milly wear artist smocks and berets if possible. If not they will be suitably dressed in their own dresses with the addition of fancy aprons. Dick should wear his own dark trousers with shirt, warm jacket or sweater, and bus driver's cap. When the cap is difficult to obtain he may wear something that looks like a ski cap. Dr. Healem wears a white or light green washable jacket. Over this he wears an overcoat, which he removes and puts on the foot of the cot when he examines Santa Claus. Paramedics wear dark blue trousers and shirts as nearly the same color as possible. Mrs. Corlett wears her mother's dress, coat, and hat. Suzette and Lynne wear their own dresses, sweaters or jackets, and hoods or caps.

The only properties are the cot, work table, and stools. The set will better suggest Santa's house if you add some Christmas decorations. Appropriate are red paper Christmas bells, big cutouts of Santa and reindeer, stars cut from gold paper, and a Christmas wreath. If you can arrange to have a window near the door, paint it to look as if there was snow on the window ledge.

The Christmas Party

by Maxine McSweeny

CHARACTERS:

GRANDMA COLLINS
HORACE COLLINS, her son
RUFENA COLLINS, his wife
MARNIE,
  age eight
                their daughters
SISSIE,
  age ten
EPHRAM HAPGOOD, agent for
  Howell's Wholesale Company

HENRY LOMASTER, a farmer
  whose crop failed
MRS. LOMASTER, his wife
MILLIE, age eight, their daughter
JIM HORNE, a newly arrived
  farmer
CLARA HORNE, his wife
ALEC, age six, their son

TIME: *The day before Christmas in any year since America has had country stores, and since American children began hanging their stockings on Christmas Eve.*

SCENE: *A country store on one of the back roads of America. Up center is a door leading to the living quarters of the Collins family. To the right of the door on the upstage wall is a fireplace. Grandma's chair is in front of the right side of the fireplace. Down right is an entrance that leads outdoors. Along the left wall and two feet from it is a counter. Behind the counter are shelves holding general merchandise, as bolts of cloth, kitchen utensils, and garden tools. From the top shelf hangs a sign,* UNITED STATES POST OFFICE. *On one end of the counter is a ball of twine. Scattered about counter and floor are containers such as wooden boxes, kegs, and cans. Homemade signs label the contents* VINEGAR, CORN MEAL, MOLASSES, *etc.*

AT RISE: *A bell jingles off right as though it were attached to an outer door. Sissie enters. She walks slowly across the stage to the counter. Marnie follows quickly and tags her.*

MARNIE: Tag, Sissie! You're it. (*Turns to run, but seeing Sissie does not turn to give chase, she hesitates.*) I tagged you.

SISSIE (*lost in her own thoughts*): I know you did.

MARNIE: Why don't you run?
SISSIE: I don't want to play.
MARNIE: Are you mad?
SISSIE: No.
MARNIE: What's the matter?
SISSIE: I wish we could have the party.
MARNIE: Maybe we will.
SISSIE: It's almost time, and Mama hasn't said a word about it.

MARNIE (*matter of factly*): Well, how can you have a party with nothing but cornbread and molasses? Who would come?

SISSIE: I would. I want it even if we don't have anything to eat. Just the singing and dancing. What will people do if Mama doesn't ask them to stay?

MARNIE: You mean when they come for their mail?

SISSIE:	Yes, the way she always does on Christmas Eve. (*Grandma enters up center. She walks slowly and leans on her cane. She shivers and draws her shawl close about her.*)
GRANDMA:	Where is that cold coming from? Is the outside door open?
MARNIE:	Yes, Grandma. I'll close it when I go.
GRANDMA:	Better close it right now. A draft is diptheria to me.
MARNIE:	All right. Just a minute. (*She runs off right where voices are heard immediately.*)

MRS. LOMASTER (*off right*): Marnie, is your papa here?
MARNIE (*off right*): Yes, Mrs. Lomaster. He's in the back.
MRS. LOMASTER (*entering hesitantly and speaking to Grandma*): Good day, Mrs. Collins.

GRANDMA:	Good day, Mrs. Lomaster. Come over here to the fire. Sissie, tell your papa Mrs. Lomaster is here. (*Sissy goes off up center. Grandma speaks to Mrs. Lomaster.*) Cold, isn't it?

MRS. LOMASTER: Yes. It feels like snow. (*She warms herself at the fire. Marnie and Millie Lomaster enter and cross left.*)

MARNIE:	You want to play tag, Millie?
MILLIE:	Yes. (*Tags Marnie.*) Tag, you're it.

MRS. LOMASTER (*interrupting their game*): Better not. (*Goes toward them.*) You might knock something over.
(*Millie and Marnie obediently sit on a box and talk.*)

MILLIE: Are you going to have the party?
MARNIE (*looks to see if anyone is listening*): I don't know.

MILLIE: It's almost time. (*They talk quietly as Horace enters up center and goes behind counter.*)

HORACE: Mrs. Lomaster, good morning. What can I do for you?

MRS. LOMASTER: Good day, Mr. Collins. I don't want much—just a little cornmeal. We're about out of everything.

HORACE (*cheerfully*): And so am I. But I do have cornmeal.

MRS. LOMASTER (*holding a piece of bright wool*): Could you take this wool for pay?

HORACE (*takes the wool and looks at it*) That's nice weaving.

MRS. LOMASTER: Would it pay for five pounds of meal?

HORACE: It's worth more than that, but I'm short of money. Could you pay just a few cents in cash?

MRS. LOMASTER (*taking wool and turning away*): No. No, I can't.

HORACE (*quickly reaching for the wool*): Here! That's all right. Maybe I can sell the wool for cash. Wait. I'll get your meal. (*He bends behind the counter, and almost immediately stands up again and calls Marnie.*)
Oh, Marnie, look what I found. There were three peppermints left in this candy bucket. Here. One for you, one for Millie, and where is Sissie?

MARNIE (*gives one to Millie, pops hers into her mouth, and runs up center*): Sissie! Come quick. Papa found a peppermint.

SISSIE (*running in*): A peppermint? Where?

HORACE (*giving peppermint to Sissie*): Here. (*to Mrs. Lomaster*) I'll get the meal.

SISSIE (*calling after him*): Oh, Papa! Thanks. A pink one. (*Puts it in her mouth*) It makes me feel Christmassy.

MARNIE: Open your mouth, Sissie. (*Breathes through her mouth*) It's hot and cold all at once. (*Sissie tries this with delight. Millie just looks at her peppermint, then smells it as if it were rare perfume.*)

GRANDMA (*tenderly watching the girls*): Millie, don't you like your peppermint?

MILLIE (*in ecstasy*): Oh, yes!

GRANDMA: Then why don't you eat it?

MILLIE: If I eat it I won't have anything in my stocking tomorrow morning.

HORACE (*returning in time to hear what Millie has just said, he listens, then turns to Mrs. Lomaster.*): It's a hard year for the children.

MRS. LOMASTER: Yes. We don't mind for ourselves. But for them—(*She presses her lips firmly together and shakes her head*)—m-mmm.

HORACE (*gently*): Here's the meal. (*He hands her the package he has just brought in.*)

MRS. LOMASTER: Thank you. Thank you, Mr. Collins. I hope you get cash for the wool.

HORACE: Don't worry about it.

MRS. LOMASTER: Well, I must go. I guess—I guess we'll be back before the mail comes.

HORACE (*embarrassed*): Yes—yes, everybody comes about that time.

MRS. LOMASTER: Come Millie. We'll go now. (*Goes off right. Millie follows carefully holding her peppermint and turning just before she goes.*)

MILLIE: I hope you have the party.
(*All others are quiet for an instant after she leaves*)
SISSIE: Papa! (*He doesn't move.*) Papa!
HORACE (*turning slowly to face her*): What, child?
SISSIE: Can't we have the singing even if we don't have the party?
HORACE: You'll have to ask your mother.
SISSIE: She'll just say to ask you.
(*Sissy and Marnie go off up center.*)
GRANDMA: Times are pretty hard, aren't they, Horace?
HORACE: Harder than you know, Ma. Harder than you know.
GRANDMA: You mean you can't pay the bills?
HORACE: I mean we're about to lose the store. I can't pay for the stock I bought last summer. Howell's are apt to take over any day.
GRANDMA: They ought to give you more time. No one can pay you. There wasn't a crop in the whole county.
HORACE: Even when they pay, it's not cash. (*Holds up Mrs. Lomaster's piece of wool.*) I can't pay Howell's with this. They want hard cash.
GRANDMA: Well, Horace, you've done as well as anyone could.
HORACE: Oh, I shouldn't have bought all that stock last summer. But crops looked fine then. I thought the farmers 'd have a jingle in their pockets. I'm just a failure at keeping store.
GRANDMA: Now, Horace, you know there's more to keeping store than buying and tying and counting the money. That cornmeal you

The Christmas Party

bought is keeping many of us alive. Some of the neighbors are living on cornmeal and creek water. Without you they'd have nothing but the water.

HORACE: Well, we're all going to suffer for my mistakes.

GRANDMA: Mistakes! Look at the mistakes your Pa made when he had the store. Remember the time he bought all those tops?

HORACE (*smiling*): Yes. Hundreds of them.

GRANDMA: Nobody played with tops any more, but we didn't know it. We thought they were a bargain.

HORACE: I wonder what Pa ever did with them. He never sold any. They were the worst stickers we ever had.

RUFENA (*entering up center followed by Marnie and Sissie, who stand dejectedly near the entrance*): Horace, why did you tell the girls to ask me about the party. You know we can't have it.

HORACE: I thought you might find a way.

RUFENA: With cornmeal and molasses for refreshments? What kind of party would that be?

HORACE: Well, nobody has anything better at home.

RUFENA: The Horne family has.

HORACE: Yes. Hornes are newcomers. They don't know what it is to plant a crop and care for it all summer and then watch it dry up.

RUFENA: I won't have Clara Horne looking down her nose at us—with cornmeal and molasses at a Christmas party.

HORACE: Well, it could be our last party. The man from Howell's Wholesale could come any time.

RUFENA: I can't believe it.
HORACE: It's true. But it doesn't need to spoil tonight. Now, everybody'll come soon to wait for the mail. We can sing the way we always do, and have some dancing. (*During this speech Sissie and Marnie move toward their father as though to support him in his plea for the party.*)
SISSIE: Please, Mama.
MARNIE: Pretty please.
RUFENA: You make it sound all right. But I can't stand the thought of it. And I'm sick of making cornbread.
MARNIE: It tasted funny today, Mama. Did it burn?
RUFENA (*almost at the breaking point*): No. It didn't burn. It just stuck to the pan. It didn't burn, and we'll eat the rest of it for supper.
GRANDMA: Suppose I make the rest of it into a pudding.
RUFENA (*her anger almost breaking out*): We're going to have that cornbreak just as it is. I'm sick of the whole thing. (*She hurries off center.*) (*The outside bell jingles. Clara Horne and Alec enter right.*)
CLARA: Merry Christmas! Merry Christmas, everybody.
HORACE (*without much enthusiasm*): Merry Christmas, Mrs. Horne.
GRANDMA: It's pretty cold out, isn't it, Clara?
CLARA: Hello, Grandma. Yes, it is cold.
ALEC (*to everybody who will listen*): You know what? (*Pause*) I got a nickel. (*Holds it up.*) I can buy anything I want.
CLARA: Alec! Not so noisy! Mr. Collins, I'm trying

The Christmas Party

	to make it seem like Christmas out here in this lonely country. I want to buy a pound of hard candy and a pound of peppermints and a pound of walnuts.
MARNIE:	If we had that we'd eat it ourselves, wouldn't we, Papa?
CLARA (*paying no attention to Marnie*):	And I want a good price because I'll pay cash. Jim said to me this morning, he said, "Clara, cash'll talk out here. You should get a lot for your money." (*Horace doesn't answer.*) May I see the candy?
HORACE:	I haven't any candy.
ALEC:	Yes you have. I saw Millie Lomaster with a peppermint. She got it here.
CLARA:	What do you mean, Mr. Collins?
HORACE:	I found three peppermints left in a candy bucket. I didn't know there was anything in it. I gave them to Millie and my girls a few minutes ago.
CLARA:	What about the hard candy, then?
HORACE:	I haven't any kind of candy.
CLARA:	Well, what'll Christmas be without candy? I guess I'll just take the walnuts. And I want a good price.
HORACE:	I don't have any walnuts, Mrs. Horne — not at any price.
CLARA:	What DO you have?
HORACE:	Not much. Some vinegar in that keg. I've got cream of tartar and soda and cornmeal and molasses.
CLARA:	Well, I did want something special for Christmas.
HORACE:	You've got more than anybody around here, Mrs. Horne.

ALEC (*wanting attention*): You know what? (*Everybody listens*) I'm going to get a stocking full of candy. (*He keeps tossing his nickel into the air and catching it while he talks.*)

CLARA: No you're not, Alec. There isn't any candy.

ALEC (*matter of fact at first, then growing angry*): Yes there is. I saw it. You gave candy to the girls. You have to give it to me. It isn't fair. (*He jumps up and down in a temper tantrum and drops his nickel. It rolls through a crack in the floor. He screams*) You've got my nickel! My nickel! It's in your floor. Now, don't give it to the girls. My nickel! My nickel!

(*Horace and Clara try to calm him. He has become so angry he can't speak. He just shakes his fists. Horace catches him under the arms to try to propel him outside. Alec hangs in his arms, a dead weight.*)

GRANDMA: Sissie! Marnie! Come here. Go down cellar and look for Alec's nickel.

SISSIE: Papa won't let us go down cellar.

GRANDMA: Go this time, anyway. Be careful, but go. Walk straight ahead from the steps to the wall. The nickel should be right there. A nickel's a lot of money this year. Ask your mother for a candle, and don't give up until you find the nickel.

MARNIE: Sissie! We get to go down cellar.

SISSY: We'll find it, Grandma.

GRANDMA: Hurry!

CLARA (*still struggling with Alec*): Come on, Alec. Come on home. Don't you hear me, Alec? I said,

The Christmas Party

come home. Do you want me to go without you?

ALEC (*still hanging limply in Horace's hands*): No! No! I want my nickel. I want my candy!

HORACE: I'll get him started home. (*Still holding Alec under the arms, Horace walks the boy out the door. Clara follows.*)

CLARA (*talking as they go*): Alec, you're a naughty boy. I've a good mind to spank you. Mr. Collins ought to spank you. (*She goes off right.*)

RUFENA (*entering up center having heard Alec's tantrum*): What's the matter?

GRANDMA: Oh, just Alec.

RUFENA (*too concerned with her own problems to ask more about Alec*): Grandma, I'm sorry I was cross about the pudding.

GRANDMA: That's all right, Rufena. You blow off steam at me any time it helps. I want to help.

RUFENA: You do help, Grandma. All the time. You give us courage. And if I ever needed courage I need it today. Everybody wants that party. What do you think of a party with cornbread and molasses?

GRANDMA (*slowly as if thinking*): Well, I guess we could think of something besides our stomachs.

(*Before Rufena can answer, the outside bell jingles, and Ephram Hapgood enters right.*)

EPHRAM (*looking around*): Hm—well—hm. Is this the Collins General store?

RUFENA: Yes, it is. Why do you ask?

EPHRAM: Well, I don't see any sign but the post office.

RUFENA: We don't need a sign. We're the only store for thirty miles. Everybody knows we're the store.
EPHRAM: Hmm—well—hm. I presume so. Anyway I want to see Mr. Collins. Is he here?
RUFENA: Grandma, do you know where Horace is?
GRANDMA: He helped Mrs. Horne get Alec home, but it wouldn't take this long. He must have come in the back.
RUFENA (*going up center and calling*): Horace! Horace!
HORACE (*off center*): What is it?
RUFENA: A man wants to see you.
(*Rufena joins Grandma at the fireplace. Horace enters up center.*)
HORACE: Good day. Can I do something for you?
EPHRAM: Plenty, Mr. Collins, plenty. (*Hands his card to Horace.*) Here's my card and connection.
HORACE: So you're Mr. Hapgood?
EPHRAM (*almost as if addressing a public meeting*): Ephram Hapgood from Howell's Wholesale Company—Collector, Buyer, and General Representative.
HORACE: I didn't look for you right at Christmas.
EPHRAM: I didn't want to be here right at Christmas.
HORACE: I'm worried about the money I owe Howell's.
EPHRAM: Howell's are worried too. Howell's said, "We're just scraping the barrel to get along. We've got to collect the bills." And I told them—I said, "Just send Ephram Hapgood. If the money's there Ephram will get it." Now, Mr. Collins, can you pay what you owe Howell's?

HORACE:	I can't pay a cent. Crops dried up here and left everybody broke. Most of the stock I bought is still on the shelf.
EPHRAM:	Maybe, you didn't buy right. A stock well-bought is a stock half-sold.
HORACE:	I sell what I can—most of it on credit or traded for some little trinket.
EPHRAM:	That's bad business. Cash is king, Mr. Collins. Cash is king.
HORACE:	Nobody has cash. If the farmers had money they'd buy for their families.
EPHRAM:	Hm—well—hmm, I don't know about that. I'm a single man, myself. Mr. Howell says to me, "Ephram, you're married to your job—just married to your job."
HORACE:	If you had children you'd know. I wish I had some little things for parents around here to put in the Christmas stockings.
EPHRAM:	Oh, you don't make much on little things.
HORACE:	Well, I'd make a lot of happiness.
EPHRAM:	Making happiness won't save the store. If you can't pay your bill, I've got to take over.
HORACE:	How much time will you give me, Mr. Hapgood?
EPHRAM:	You've had six months. Howell's can't wait any longer. I've got to take over the store now.

RUFENA (*stepping toward him*): Now!! You mean today?
EPHRAM: Yes, today. I hope I don't spoil your Christmas.
RUFENA (*unbelieving at first, then with firm resolve walking so close to Ephram he keeps stepping back*): Don't worry Mr. Hapgood. You

won't spoil Christmas. Take the store if that's your duty, but you can't take Christmas. For ten years we've had a party Christmas Eve. We've always had good food and a good time. Well, this year we can't have the good food, but in spite of you and Howell's and bad crops, we'll have the good time—same as always.

HORACE (*jubilant*): Rufena! I knew you'd do it.

RUFENA (*smiling at Horace*): Horace, I'm going to the kitchen now. I want to mix a big batch of cornbread for the party. (*She goes off up center.*)

EPHRAM (*catching his breath after listening to Rufena's outburst.*): Well—hmm—well. Go ahead. Have your party. But you can't have it here.

HORACE: It has to be here. It's the only place there is.

EPHRAM: You can't come partying around this stock. It might get damaged. (*Takes a big padlock from his pocket.*) I've got to lock up the store. (*He moves toward outside door.*)

GRANDMA: Wait a minute, Mr. Hapgood. How'll people get their mail?

EPHRAM: I don't know how they'll get their mail. (*He is taking a key from his pocket to open the padlock.*) That's not my business.

GRANDMA: You know, Mr. Hapgood, this store is more than a store. It's a United States Post Office.

HORACE: That's right Mr. Hapgood. See the sign? You can't padlock the post office.

GRANDMA:	That would be interfering with the mail.
HORACE:	It's a federal crime.
GRANDMA:	You might go to prison.
EPHRAM	(*He has been looking from one to the other as if watching a tennis match while their speeches have followed each other in rapid succession*): Hmm—well—hmm—well, I don't want to interfere with the mail.
GRANDMA:	Of course you don't. Now, Mr. Hapgood, forget about locking up for tonight. Just come to the party. You and I—we'll both watch the stock. Just come to the party and have a good time. (*Bell jingles.*) Someone's coming now. (*Ephram goes behind the counter and examines the stock on the shelves. Enter Clara and Jim Horne followed by Alec and Millie Lomaster. Behind them are Mrs. Lomaster and her husband, Henry.*)
HORACE:	Merry Christmas, all of you.
MILLIE:	Oh, Merry Christmas, Mr. Collins.
HENRY:	Hello, Horace.
JIM:	Good evening, Horace.
MRS. LOMASTER:	Merry Christmas to you, Mr. Collins.
CLARA:	I'm back again, Mr. Collins. (*Greetings are friendly, but they are not gay or hearty. Mrs. Lomaster goes to Grandma.*)
ALEC (*to everybody*):	Did you find my nickel?
JIM:	Alec! Quiet! (*He takes Alec's hand and holds him close. Alec understands and is silent.*)
HENRY:	We're a little early, Horace.
JIM:	We heard about your Christmas parties,

	and we didn't want to miss anything.
CLARA:	Oh, Jim! Maybe there won't be "anything" this year.
	(*Millie moves toward Horace and watches him as she waits for his answer.*)
HORACE:	Yes. There will, Clara. Same as always.
MILLIE:	Oh, Mr. Collins! (*runs to her mother*) Mama! Mama! We're going to have the party.
HORACE:	Jim, will you and Henry give me a hand here? (*They move kegs and boxes to clear center stage.*)
JIM:	Glad to.
HENRY:	Here. Let me take this.
HORACE:	(*to Clara*): Rufena's in the kitchen. She's mixing the cornbread.
CLARA:	My! I'll be glad to taste Rufena's cornbread.
	(*She starts up center but stops when Rufena enters there. Rufena is wiping her hands on her apron.*)
RUFENA:	Merry Christmas! Merry Christmas. I'm glad all of you came.
	(*There follows a jumble of greetings. Horace goes to the counter.*)
HORACE:	Mr. Hapgood! Come! Join the party. This is Mr. Hapgood from the city.
EPHRAM (*shaking hands with Henry, who stands nearest*): How do you do?
	(*Before Henry or anyone else can greet Mr. Hapgood Marnie and Sissie call from offstage, up center "Mama! "Mama!" They enter, each one carrying a top.*)
MARNIE (*holding out the top*): Mama, look what we found.

The Christmas Party

SISSIE (*seeing the guests and looking questioningly at her mother*): Mama? Papa? Is it the party?
RUFENA: It is, child. The Christmas party.
MARNIE (*in wonder and gratitude*): Same as always.
RUFENA: Except refreshments. They're just cornbread and molasses. But we have our good neighbors and the same old goodwill.
SISSY (*beaming*): Goodwill! Peace and goodwill! Mama, you sound like the angels.
MARNIE: But the angels didn't say anything about cornbread.
HORACE: That's all right, Marnie. Mr. Hapgood, these are our daughters, Marnie and Sissie. (*The girls smile and nod.*)
EPHRAM: How do you do. (*Reaches for Marnie's top.*) What's this?
SISSIE (*handing her top to Horace*): What is it, Papa? We found a box full of them down cellar.
MARNIE: But we didn't find Alec's nickel.
ALEC: My nickel! (*He bounds forward but is immediately seized and silenced by his father.*)
JIM: Alec! Quiet!
HORACE (*taking the top*): You found the tops. (*Holds it up*) Look, Ma, look! They found Pa's tops.
GRANDMA: Let me see. (*Sissie takes the top to her. Grandma holds it tenderly.*) Your Pa's tops.
EPHRAM (*breaking a piece of string from the ball on the counter he winds the top*): First top I've seen in twenty years. I used to be a champion. (*He spins the top on the counter.*) Watch it go.

EPHRAM: (*The spectators are delighted. There are cries of "Look at it go." "Watch it spin." "Let me see." As the top begins to waver Ephram triumphantly scoops it up.*) Mr. Collins, these tops could be the biggest selling toy in the country. I want Howell's to be first with them. Will you sell me that box of tops?

HORACE: Of course. That's what I'm here for. (*Notices the children*) Only—only I have to keep a few. These children have to find tops in their Christmas stockings tomorrow morning.

MILLIE: Oh, Mr. Collins! A peppermint AND a top!

HORACE (*smiles at Millie, then turns quickly to Ephram*): But I can sell you two or three hundred.

EPHRAM: That'll be payment on the bill you owe Howell's.

RUFENA: Then you won't have to close the store?

EPHRAM: Not if I get the tops.

HORACE: You'll get them. But you forget something. These tops are just a drop in the bucket. You can sell a boxful like mine to every storekeeper from here to Chicago. Where will you get enough tops?

EPHRAM: Hmm—well—hm. I have to figure that out.

HORACE: I've got it all figured. We can whittle tops. We're good at it. Some of us like Henry Lomaster are as good as wood carvers. Anybody who can't whittle tonight'll learn by New Years. We can whittle tops until spring planting.

EPHRAM: It's a deal, Mr. Collins.
(*The others, silent until now, break into excited conversation. Everybody talks:*
ALL: Whittle tops? Can you whittle? So can I. We'll make the little spinners. Will you teach me? Sure!
HORACE (*holding up his hand for silence*): Wait a minute. Remember, Mr. Hapgood, everybody here needs money. When will you pay us?
EPHRAM: I told you cash was king. I'll pay cash on delivery.
HORACE: Good enough!
ALL: Cash on delivery! Real money! Can you believe it? When do we begin? Right now.
HORACE: Now, let's begin the party. Rufena!
(*He takes her hand and starts singing, "Jolly Is the Miller." They lead all others into a circle. Mr. and Mrs. Lomaster are the next couple. Following them are Jim and Clara Horne, Marnie and Sissie, and Ephram and Millie. Alec gets in the middle of the circle to play "Miller." Grandma claps her hands to the rhythm of the song. Everybody sings with great heartiness as all play the game, "Jolly Is the Miller." At its end Horace and Rufena lead all off up center. Grandma is last to go. She sings and taps her cane although she moves slowly. The singing continues until she disappears after the others.*)

[THE END]

SUGGESTIONS FOR THE DIRECTOR

Regarding Rehearsal and Production of *The Christmas Party*
Here is a play for a group of young teenage boys and girls. It offers eleven good parts for them to act. The play has no starring roles, but many good ones. The lines are so well divided among the characters, and each character is so necessary to the story that every player has reason to feel his part important. The three smallest girls of the group should be cast as Sissie, Marnie, and Millie. Although these players may be teenagers they can be convincing as children if they are shorter than those who play adults. However, the part of Alec should be played by a younger child. The part offers so much fun for the boy who plays it that there should be no difficulty in recruiting a young brother or friend for the role.

Before directing this play you should realize that interest in it comes from something other than dashing movement or physical conflict. Audience interest in the play will come from its feeling for the characters and its desire to know what happens to them. This means that from the beginning you should help players make their characters so vital that the audience lives with them their trials and triumphs. To make the play exciting you plan how to sharpen contrasts and suspense throughout the performance. You want to keep the audience wondering how it will all come out.

At the first rehearsal you help players get the feeling for the characters they are enacting. Immediately following a cast reading of the play, assemble the players in an intimate group for discussion. Focus their thoughts on the disaster that has befallen the storekeeper, the farmers, and their families. They spent their money to buy seed; they worked hard to prepare the ground, plant the seed, care for the young plants. Then came the drought, which dried the plants so there was no grain to harvest.

Induce the players to think about these hardships and their effects on the residents of the little farm community. Ask questions like these:

    Did the crops fail because farmers were lazy and neglected the plants?
    Is the store failing because Horace has not taken care of his business?
    Is there anyone to whom these people can turn for help?
    Do they show courage in the face of hardship, or do they whine and complain and criticize one another?
    What causes the parents their greatest suffering?
    Do you like these people because of the way they accept adversity?
    Are they ready to give up?

Allow time for discussion of answers to each question. Let players answer first with their opinions, then back up their opinions with quotations from the script. Such discussion helps players think about the motives and emotions of characters before trying to learn to speak lines in the script. Throughout rehearsals remind players to consider why characters speak as they do, then to show these reasons to the audience.

Also throughout rehearsals you should guide players so they develop sharp contrasts and steadily growing suspense. To equip yourself to give such guidance, mark in your script all the moments that serve these purposes. To contrast with the gloom that pervades the little country neighborhood, mark all of the cheerful moments in the play. Then mark the moments that provide lively emotional excitement even if they are not happy moments. Perhaps, most important of all, mark the moments that are important in telling the play's story, in making the audience wonder what will happen next, and hope that everything turns out well.

The first bright moment occurs when Marnie enters just after the play begins. Sissie has already come in worried and despondent. With her manner she has established the prevailing atmosphere. Marnie, a younger child, does not realize how desperate the little community is. All she wants at the moment is a game. In the hope of playing tag she runs or skips or does a combination of them. She might well be singing a snatch of a singing game like "The Farmer in the Dell" or "Looby Loo." She sings with gusto until she tags Sissie. Then she turns and runs. Give her time and space for big movement. Not until she reaches the entrance does she look back to see why Sissie does not give chase. Suggest to Marnie that she take time to show how her feelings change from happy anticipation to, first, awareness that Sissie is not playing, and then, to curiosity as to what ails Sissie. Marnie's first explanation to herself must be that Sissie does not realize she was tagged. That is why Marnie says simply, "I tagged you." Two speeches later Marnie is amazed at Sissie's answer, "I don't want to play." Marnie must show her surprise in order to let the audience know that the two girls are accustomed to join in happy games. Marnie can make the surprise conspicuous by taking a few steps toward Sissie before asking, "Are you mad?"

Such a movement can also add suspense. It gives the audience time to wonder why Sissie won't play. It is ready to listen when she answers with the line that begins to reveal the plot. The play's action begins to rise when Sissie says, "I wish we could have the party." From that instant players should keep the audience wondering whether there will be a party.

One way to do this is for every character except Rufena to mention the party with a look and tone of voice that shows the joy of past parties and the desire for one tonight. Before players speak the word *party*, their eyes tell how much they want it. Sissie shows this in her first speeches.

A few minutes later Millie shows the same when she asks Marnie, "Are you going to have the party?" To emphasize her desire she pauses after the word *have*. In this short pause she looks around like a child seeing her first Christmas tree. Then with awed delight she says, "the party."

In the same scene Mrs. Lomaster refers to the party without daring to utter the word. Hesitantly she says, "I guess — I guess we'll be coming in before the mail comes." She thinks about the party, hopes for it, but dares not ask. Pauses give her a chance to show longing, one pause after the first "I guess" to show embarrassment. She pauses again after "in" to look into the distance and smile at the memory of past parties. Then still remembering she slowly speaks the rest of the sentence.

The scene with Millie and her mother not only accentuates the general longing for the party. It provides the relief of some happy moments. The first is Millie's short-lived game of tag with Marnie. Even though it is short, make it gay. The two girls run and squeal with the joy of the game. Their quick steps and hearty shouts are pleasing contrast to the worried sadness of Grandma and Mrs. Lomaster. The children make enough noise to attract Mrs. Lomaster's attention. Before she speaks she shows her concern that Millie might damage something in the store.

Then comes the happiest moment of the first half of the play. Horace finds the peppermints. The ecstasy of the children over a mere peppermint apiece shows how rare their treats have been. Let each girl revel in looking at her peppermint, feeling it, smelling it, tasting, and finally, eating it.

As the scene ends, Millie's parting words bring back the thought of the party. She turns as she leaves to say, "I hope you have the party." Her naturally cheerful disposition makes her more optimistic than others are. She shows this by the sprightly way she speaks.

The joy of the peppermint scene makes all the graver the scene that follows when Horace tells Grandma he may lose the store. From here on, the audience should have reason to worry about the store as well as the party. Suspense will be increased if Grandma shows shocked dismay at Horace's news. And Horace shows his disappointment by his posture, his gesture, and his eyes as well as by his words.

Then comes the speech that foreshadows the solution to all the problems. In trying to comfort Horace, Grandma mentions the tops. How can she say it so the audience will note and remember the tops? She could highlight the idea if on the beginning of the speech she got up and paced back and forth. Her reason for getting up is agitation over the plight of the store. She paces while saying, "Look at the mistakes your Pa made when he had the store." Then suddenly she stops pacing, smiles at her thought, and turns to Horace. Only after this movement does she say, "Remember the time he bought all those tops." Horace smiles too as he says, "Yes." Together their mood changes to one of happy reminiscing about Pa. But almost immediately Horace comes back to reality. He should show this with some change in his body position as he says, "I wonder what he ever did with them." This lets the audience know the tops might be someplace near.

Their conversation is interrupted by Rufena. She brings again the worry about the party. Horace shows his longing for it when he says, "I thought you might find a way." Then he pleads, "It may be our last." His inflection on the word **last** conveys his love of the parties. Then he makes some quick movement to show change of thought and mood before he says "The man from Howell's Wholesale could come any time."

In contrast to Horace's calmness Rufena has almost reached the breaking point. She shows this with the quality of her voice, quick gestures, and restless movement about the stage.

Then comes a lively if not exactly a happy diversion. Alec enters. Spoiled and pampered he is a contrast to the girls. Let his anger grow slowly when he learns there is no candy. Then he explodes in a tantrum when he loses his nickel. His mother's inabilaity to control him may provide a little humor.

When Alec drops the nickel be sure it disappears. He should let it fall behind one of the boxes on the floor so the audience has no chance to see what actually becomes of it. Spectators see only the reaction of players as dumbfounded they watch while the nickel presumably rolls through a crack in the floor. Practice with a real nickel, and stress the need for intense watching and big reaction on the part of all players present.

The performance should pick up speed as Grandma tells the girls to search the cellar for the nickel. This faster tempo is another contrast since the early part of the play moved slowly.

With the entrance of Ephram Hapgood comes a character who contrasts with the natives of the little community. Ephram is flushed with his success and responsibility. His manner shows how pleased he is with himself. He is so complacent as he says, "I hope I don't spoil your Christmas" that Rufena turns on him.

You should make this moment vivid. With the first shock at Ephram's comment she steps back in horror. Then her long-smouldering frustration breaks forth. She hammers home to him the good word that she will have the party. It is Ephram's turn to back away. Like a hammer she approaches him again and again to make it plain that he can't spoil Christmas. The shocked reaction of Horace and Grandma increases the excitement of the scene. Then Horace grows jubilant at Rufena's decision to have the party. Grandma's pleasure is obvious but more quietly expressed.

Another suspenseful moment occurs with Ephram's declaration that he will padlock the store. Increase this suspense by having Horace take time to show his dismay as he realizes the party is again in jeopardy. Then Grandma gets an idea. She must take time to show she has the idea *before* she speaks. This gives the audience time and reason to wonder what will happen. Quietly but with determination Grandma rescues the party when she says, "Wait a minute, Mr. Hapgood."

Relief from tension follows as the farmers and their families enter. They are not merry, but they have the pleasure of being together for the party. Marnie brings a genuinely happy moment when she enters and sees they are having the party. She should look all around the room and show her delight before she says, "Same as always."

When Ephram spins the top the adults show a nostalgic pleasure. The children watch fascinated. There is a general flurry of excitement while the top spins, then intense concentration when Ephram mentions buying the tops. Solutions to the play's problems come fast from here on. After Ephram says, "That'll be a payment on what you owe Howell's" Horace shows relief in both face and body. Then he says, "Then you won't have to close the store?"

All who are present should show at least momentary pleasure in Horace's good fortune. Their interest in him grows intense as he tells Ephram that everyone there can make tops. No one moves or makes a sound. All look at Horace and listen to what he says. When Ephram announces, "Cash on delivery," general rejoicing begins. At first it takes the form of muttered exclamations of disbelief, then of wonder, and finally, shouts of joy. It reaches a climax as the singing and dancing begin.

The play's costumes and stage sets are determined by the era in which you decide the action occurs. The suggestions in the script are for the end of the nineteenth century or beginning of the twentieth. Several effective productions have used this period. Those who chose this era found items of costume and set were easy to obtain and of interest to the audience.

The women wore long dresses with fitted bodices and gathered skirts. Over Rufena's dress was a long apron. Grandma and women who came from outside wore shawls. The girls' dresses were similar to their mothers' but shorter. They wore long, black, cotton stockings. Marnie and Sissie had aprons, and Millie, a jacket. A kerchief was tied over Millie's head and under her chin. Each girl's hair hung in two neat braids down her back. Sissie had a black ribbon bow low on the back of her head.

Men's costumes were overalls, not jeans, but overalls with bibs and shoulder straps. Jim and Henry wore plaid jackets and caps with earmuffs. Over his overalls Horace wore a plain black apron cut like a butcher's apron. Ephram's business suit was worn under an overcoat. When he entered he took off the coat. He also wore a cap with earmuffs. Taking off the cap and coat provided him with good business as soon as he came in. Alec had the same kind of cap as the men's. The rest of his costume was composed of knickers, jacket, and long, coarsely ribbed, black stockings.

To add interesting details to the set a cotton print curtain was hung over the upstage entrance. A counter was created with planks on saw horses. (If you don't have these, line up a row of apple boxes, and cover the top and front of them with long strips of butcher paper.)

For the bell that rings when any one opens the offstage outside door, select one that makes a sound loud enough to attract attention. This sound will be particularly helpful in getting the audience settled and attentive on Sissie's entrance at the beginning of the play.